THE ANTS ARE MY FRIENDS

THE ANTS ARE MY FRIENDS

Misheard Lyrics, Malapropisms,
Eggcorns, and other linguistic gaffes

MARTIN TOSELAND

PORTICO

First published in the United Kingdom in 2007 by
Portico Books
10 Southcombe Street
London
W14 0RA

An imprint of Anova Books Company Ltd

ISBN 9781906032067

A CIP catalogue record for this book is available from the British Library.

10 9 8 7 6 5 4 3 2 1

Typeset by SX Composing DTP, Rayleigh, Essex
Printed and bound by WS Bookwell, Finland

This book can be ordered direct from the publisher.
Contact the marketing department, but try your bookshop first.

www.anovabooks.com

contents

ACKNOWLEDGEMENTS

A huge thank you to my publisher Tom Bromley who has been very calm about a scary schedule and has had lots of very creative suggestions for the book. Thanks also to Jackie for listening to endless language mauling and still managing to be enthusiastic about it. I'm very grateful to Cathy, Fran, Dad, and Simon and Kim for their suggestions and encouragement.

P.G. Wodehouse once dedicated a book to his daughter by writing: 'To my daughter Leonora without whose never-failing sympathy and encouragement this book would have been finished in half the time.' I dedicate this book to Hannah whose delight in finding new mishearings and mis-speakings lengthened the process but made it double the fun.

INTRODUCTION

This book celebrates linguistic creativity – inadvertent creativity, usually, but creativity nevertheless. Sometimes, when we listen to a friend, a relative, or a song, our ears play tricks on us and we mishear what someone is saying or singing. This can result in just a misheard word in a phrase which we casually repeat to someone else or, at the other extreme, we start to construct a whole new narrative (say in a song) based on what we misheard. As a nine-year-old, I was convinced that Christ 'the royal Master' (in 'Onward Christian Soldiers') 'leans against the phone' watching his banners go. At the time, the picture of Him, lolling around on a street corner, propped up against a telephone box, waving the troops off, made perfect sense. On other occasions, it's the mouth that plays the trick and the wrong word just comes out. Whether we mishear or mis-speak, it is often the language as a whole that benefits. The 'mistake' proves as interesting, funny or evocative as the original word, phrase or lyric. *The Ants Are My Friends* is a selection of such accidental linguistic invention. The title comes from lyrics in Bob Dylan's classic protest song 'Blowin' in the Wind' which are sometimes misheard as a confession of chuminess with the little insects.

I've selected words from three categories: **malapropisms**, which is when the wrong word just comes out and as a result a funny or a just plain bizarre picture appears; **eggcorns**, which is a new linguistic term coined for those words you mishear but the misheard word is better than the original – of which more below; and finally, **mondegreens** or misheard song lyrics.

Malapropisms are famously named after the character Mrs Malaprop in Sheridan's play *The Rivals*. This 'old, weather-beaten she-dragon' truly has the gift of the gaffe or, as she might say, she represents the 'very pineapple' of linguistic blundering. The word comes from the French *mal à propos* which is roughly 'ill to purpose' or, in other words, inappropriate. But there was a rich tradition of malapropping before she appeared in 1775. Indeed the first recorded malapropism could well be in Chaucer's *The Canterbury Tales* which was finished in about 1400. The noble art is seen running through Shakespeare (particularly in the character of Dogberry in *Much Ado About Nothing*), Sheridan, Dickens and into the twentieth century when speech became widely recorded and we had first-hand access to people who mis-speak. So much so that there are now subcategories of malapropism, usually created by specific people who warrant a range of stumbles named after them. So we have the current leader of the free world fumbling around the edges of the English language, creating 'transformationed' words and expressions of troublesome meaning ('weapons of mass production'); Jade Goody giving us the benefit of her wisdom ('Where's East Angular? I thought it was abroad.'); and the rather more artful Dave Farber (an American college professor renowned for his linguistic dexterity and inventor of such phrases as, 'He won't last. He's just a flash in the pants'). Television has bought us Del Boy who seems to be fluent in malapropism not only in English but French, Spanish and Italian as well; Archie Bunker from the US sitcom *All in the Family*; and in the last few years, Sacha Baron Cohen has created Ali G and Borat, both of whom are expert manglers of English.

Sport is an area where the high passion of an occasion seems to provoke slips of the tongue. I have only included sports gaffes where they add something to the language. Often when sportsmen and sportswomen (and commentators) stumble over their words, they say something completely daft or utterly impossible. These types of mistakes were christened 'Colemanballs' by *Private Eye* and there are many books with hundreds of examples of them. Thus Bryan Robson, the former Manchester United captain, said in 1990, 'If we played like that every week we wouldn't be so inconsistent', and that is an archetypal Colemanball. However, in this book, I've concentrated on those times where the language is beaten up to the extent that something new is created. So when Martin Tyler, the football commentator, remarked that the game he was watching was 'not a game for the puritans' there is immediately an image of a group of black-and-white-clad Cromwell followers being booted off the field.

Malapropisms are sometimes provoked when a character or person is under pressure and the words they utter reveal what they think as opposed to what they meant to say. Peter Simple in *The Merry Wives of Windsor* is asked by Falstaff and Host to reveal the secret questions he has been told to ask of Mistress Page. He replies: 'I may not conceal them, sir' (IV.v.56), thereby betraying his instructions from Slender. If used intentionally in fiction and drama, they work to highlight the pomposity of the speaker to great comic effect. When used unintentionally in real life, they can do the same thing – while this is often very funny it is sometimes not that creative. I've tried to focus, here, on the creativity of malapropisms – where the mis-speaking contains a new image or idea which can be re-used or re-cycled in another situation. In other words, they are little nudges pushing the language forward or in a different direction.

'Eggcorn' is a name for a particular kind of misheard word. It was coined by linguist Mark Lieberman who came across someone who had heard 'eggcorn' in the phrase 'great oaks from little acorns grow'. Lieberman thought that 'eggcorn' was an excellent word and was just as suggestive, if not more so, that 'acorn'. From that point on, more and more of these creations appeared and a pattern of sorts emerged. The misheard word (the one being replaced) was often archaic or only used in a phrase or expression; our natural tendency is to use what is familiar to us when faced with something that is unfamiliar or unrecognisable. So, we grasp for a word we know that sounds like the one we don't know, rather than hazard a guess as to what the original might have been. Hence, we get 'chestfallen' for 'crestfallen' and 'damp squid' for 'damp squib'. When they work well, a new expression, phrase or word is born which often provides a different or extra nuance to the original version. There is a small industry now devoted to digging up these linguistic truffles and there are many excellent places to discover them – the best of which is the Eggcorns Database (http://eggcorns.lascribe.net/). The challenge with this assembling of misheard words and expressions is to catch them as they fall.

'Mondegreens' are misheard song lyrics and they, too, are a rich seam to mine for accidental invention. Given a radio and our imaginations, there is no limit to our ability to distort a song's message or words. The word 'mondegreen' was coined by an American writer Sylvia Wright in the 1950s. She wrote an essay for *Harper's Magazine* where she quoted a Scottish ballad ('The Bonnie Earl of Murray') which she had misheard when she was growing up:

Ye Highlands and ye Lowlands,
Oh, where hae ye been?
They have slain the Earl of Murray,
And Lady Mondegreen.

The last line should read 'And laid him on the green'. So Lady Mondegreen came into being and for that we should be eternally grateful.

The pictures we conjure irresistibly lead us down paths so far from the original song that we stubbornly cling to our original mishearing and mould what we subsequently hear to our invented storyline. So we adapt the relationships in the song, the attitude of the people and the singer, the location and many other details as we listen, and this is what makes collecting mondegreens such good sport. One of the best examples I've come across is the Monkees' song 'I'm a Believer'. Many have heard the line 'Then I saw her face, now I'm a believer' as 'Then I saw her face, now I'm gonna leave her'. This when in the preceding lines the singer had lamented his lack of luck in finding love. The 'mondegreenee' manages to disregard the emotional set-up of the song and accept that this previously sad, under-confident and disappointed character, desperate for any kind of romance, is now a hard-hearted, callous ingrate. Your ears do weird things to your emotional intelligence.

The moment of revelation about what the band or artist was really saying can be humiliating or funny (I'm sure it was 'We all itch in South Capri' not 'We are agents of the free' in REM's 'Orange Crush') or just irritating if you think your version is so much better – which it quite frequently is. I've included as many of these as is possible although the pool to choose from is immense. There is also a list of my top ten which have been chosen on a completely subjective basis and without any other qualification than I've been 'lucky' enough to spend a considerable time looking out for them – more time than is probably advisable for any music fan. Bands and artists whose work has been most misheard are in separate panels and I've ventured to name the lyric I think deserves the accolade of 'Most Mondegreened' of all time. If you have further examples that you like which are not in this book, please do email them to theantsaremyfriends@googlemail.com and I will continue to compile a poll to establish if there is a better or more popular example.

The Ants Are My Friends is a collection of the examples I have encountered which have most amused, entertained or intrigued me. There are panels throughout where I've put together similar examples or sources of mishear or mis-speak – so in addition to the ones mentioned above there are boxes relating to Christmas, to food and to Shakespeare and the original Mrs Malaprop. A full list is given in the next section. There is also a panel dedicated to misheard song titles – it's almost wilfully perverse to mishear the name of the song but people do and, oddly enough, these mishearings are often the most elaborate.

Kurt Cobain once sang (as far as at least one listener was concerned), 'Here we are now, we're contagious'; I hope you find this sample of linguistic creativity, addictive and entertaining.

Martin Toseland
London, March 2007

Key to Symbols

 Eggcorn

 Mondegreen

 Malapropism

Top Ten Entry

THE ANTS ARE MY FRIENDS

 He's not going to **adhere** himself to the fans.

Alan Mullery is a former Tottenham and England captain and was the first England player to be sent off in an international match; he is now a pundit for Sky Sports where generally he is gaffe-free. Mullery is often critical of modern players, though he takes it too far here by suggesting that slapping on the SuperGlue and throwing yourself at the fans is a thing to be admired. As so often with old professionals-turned-pundits, there is a further undercurrent that things ain't what they used to be; of course, in his day, the terraces at White Hart Lane were littered with old professionals stuck irrevocably to irate fans.

And now I know that I'm **adopted.**

Morrissey is not well known for talking about his private life but some listeners believe that in The Smiths' 1986 single 'Big Mouth Strikes Again' he reveals this intimate detail. Instead, he sings 'And now I know how Joan of Arc felt' which is perhaps also very self-revelatory – Morrissey as the Patron Saint of Martyrs?

The Smiths, 'Big Mouth Strikes Again'

Then he's so well bred; – so full of **alacrity, and adulation!** – and has so much to say for himself: – in such good language, too! His physiognomy so grammatical!

Mrs Malaprop's relentless mangling of English in Sheridan's *The Rivals* is exhausting as much as it is hilarious. She never speaks a true word when a wrong word will do and just when you think you are getting the gist of what she is about to say, she throws a curve-word at you. This is just one example of her art; more are assembled in 'The Original Mrs Malaprop' panel on p. 99.

Sheridan, *The Rivals*

You'll have to come up to date and have microphones, Vicar. The **agnostics** in this church are very poor.

Here, in a glorious example of the malaproptic art, the editors of *Good News* magazine cite a letter from a concerned parishioner: how can we convert the non-believers if they a) can't hear you and b) need financial aid. One wonders what the agnostics are doing in the church in the first place but what chance making them believe if they can't hear what you're saying?

***Good News* Magazine**

It's an **Alcatraz** around my neck.

Politics attracts its fair share of malapropists. Boston's Mayor Thomas Menino certainly has the gift of the gaffe. In this instance, while agreeing with journalists in the US that the shortage of parking spaces in the city was a problem, he clearly felt that it might lead to his ultimate incarceration. The bird he was looking for was of course the albatross.

Eggcorn   Malapropism   Mondegreen

The river had a thin layer of green **allergy** clinging to the surface, and huge pie-shaped figures floating upon them. It was so real.

There are moments in language where cause and effect come together and merge into a single word. This sentence from a child's story shows one such instance where the effect of the algae is plain to see in the substituted word 'allergy'. If you wanted you could swap the words around again and come up with 'I have a dust algae' which is quite neat too.

www.kidpub.org

However, as matters transpired he almost got something from the game but despite losing late on Lisselton did show a marked improvement in form and it **all goes** well for the future.

While the verb 'augur' is slipping unremarked out of usage, the platitude 'hope it all goes well for you' is becoming ubiquitous. It was only a matter of time then that the phrase shouldered its way into the space occupied by 'augur'. So, instead of having a word that conjures up images of fortune-tellers, soothsayers and the entrails of rabbits, we have the most banal of phrases taking its place.

The *Kingdom*

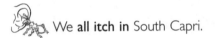 We **all itch in** South Capri.

REM's frontman Michael Stipe is up there amongst the world record holders for the number of mondegreens his singing and lyrics provoke. In 'Orange Crush' rather than being 'agents of the free', the inhabitants of the Italian island off the coast of Naples apparently have a hereditary condition – but only those on the southern tip. The beauty is in the detail.

REM, 'Orange Crush'

Eggcorn   Malapropism   Mondegreen

What me? No, no, I'm **ambiguous**!

Del Boy in *Only Fools and Horses* is a practised exponent of the noble art of malapropism. Fluent in English gaffery as well as French, Spanish and Latin, Del needs no encouragement to slip into another tongue. Here, though, he gives us a pukka English malapropism for 'ambidextrous'. (See also AMPHIBIOUS below.)

Only Fools and Horses, Cash and Curry

[When asked how he could 'shoot baskets' so well with both hands] It could be because I'm **amphibious**.

Underwater basketball anyone? The basketball player in question is one Cozell McQueen whose other claim to fame seems to be that he finished in the top ten in 'rebounding' in 1985–6 season for the Wisconsin Flyers. As Minor League Basketball in the US is an impenetrable mystery to me that fact can sit, isolated, in all its glory.

[Mr Cruncher himself always spoke of the year of our Lord as **Anna Dominoes**: apparently under the impression that the Christian era dated from the invention of a popular game, by a lady who had bestowed her name upon it.]

In which case, the years before our Lord could have been Bernard Cribbage …

Charles Dickens, *A Tale of Two Cities*

That is why I developed the appendix on the historical shortcomings of the thesis in *Mystery of Romans*. Let me share with you **antidotal** evidence for the need to provide that appendix.

While antidotes do provide evidence when they are used in trials to see how effective they are, this is a fairly specialised area of research.

🌴 Eggcorn   🍍 Malapropism   🐜 Mondegreen

Less specialised, indeed altogether unscientific, is anecdotal evidence or findings based on heresy, sorry, hearsay (see p.77). Antidotal evidence, though, might be required in the entry that follows.

lists.ibiblio.org

The cookbook is being compiled. Please submit your favourite recipe and a short **antidote** concerning it.

This example is almost too neat to be true but it is quoted by Richard Lederer who is a lifelong 'gaffemonger'. I presume that the writer intended that people send in anecdotes with their recipes; otherwise the invitation to send in an antidote make one think that perhaps the book being compiled is *The Poisoner's Cookbook*.

These are my **antipants**.

Borat describes these to a group of teenagers in Atlanta, Georgia in his film. It's a good description of the greying, string-style Y-front creation which Steve Bell always depicted John Major wearing in his cartoon strips 'If…' If you wanted a picture of what pants should not be, then look no further than 'antipants'.

Borat

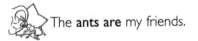

The **ants are** my friends.

Bob Dylan's 1963 protest song becomes a tribute to his insect friends according to some listeners. Instead of the 'answer' to the song's strident questions 'blowin' in the wind', there are hundreds of his ant friends being blown along, getting in everyone's way, only protected by Bob's friendship. What happens to them when he gets to the harmonica solo is not explained.

Bob Dylan, 'Blowin' in the Wind'

I don't want to cast **asparagus** at my opponents.

Nor should you. Richard Daley, former Mayor of Chicago, was famous for mangling his words. He was a habitual malaproper (see PLATITUDES and PRESERVE below) whose press secretary once told journalists, 'You should have printed what he meant, not what he said.' The world would have been a poorer place if they had taken his advice. Asparagus is, apparently, meant to be excellent at keeping you young-looking. Aside from getting a charge of assault, Daley could also have been helping preserve his opponent which doesn't make good political sense. Daley of course meant to say 'aspersions'.

 I don't know what the fellow was on about ... He kept talking about **an automatic pier.**

John Lennon loved to play with words. This deliberate mishearing of a journalist's questions about his use of *onomatopoeia* is one example – although I'm not sure what sound an automatic pier makes ...

Bb

I've got a **back ache** from loving you.

The full title of Robert Palmer's 1979 single is 'Bad Case of Loving You (Doctor, Doctor)'. In the tradition of excellent misheard song titles this one embellishes the original title and we get a rather different story emerging. Let's not even begin to think how he got his bad back but at least he is seeing a doctor about it.

Robert Palmer, 'Bad Case of Loving You'

Only **Baloney**.

Roy Orbison's 1960 hit 'Only the Lonely' comforted (or tormented, I'm never quite sure) thousands of broken-hearted teenagers. However, he never intended that they should resort to salami to get over their heartaches – Dum-dum-dum-dumdy-doo-wah.

Roy Orbison, 'Only the Lonely'

Ahoy, ahoy, **barman and soda**.

The Skids' 'Into the Valley' is one of those songs where the lyrics are so utterly indecipherable that you either murmur or la-la-la along until you get to the song title which you then belt out with as much gusto and conviction as you can muster. So, if someone comes up with a line that seems to work, cling on to it – it doesn't matter whether it is right or wrong, no one else knows the words anyway. For the record the actual lyrics for this line are, 'Ahoy, Ahoy! Boy, man and soldier'. Yep, it was a surprise to me too.

The Skids, 'Into the Valley'

There's a **bathroom** on the right.

Creedence Clearwater Revival's 1969 song 'Bad Moon Rising' is full of portents and ill-omens. There are hurricanes, earthquakes and lightning as well as rivers overflowing. So, when John Foggarty advises not to visit a certain place because it'll take your life, the expectation is that there is something symbolically dangerous outside. Instead, some people hear 'There's a bathroom on the right' as opposed to the actual line, 'There's a bad moon on the rise'. Bathrooms don't tend to be that threatening unless you're hydrophobic of course.

Creedence Clearwater Revival, 'Bad Moon Rising'

Let me drown in your **bathtub**.

If there is a more sentimental, irritating song than John Denver's 'Annie's Song', I don't want to hear it. The delight of coming across this great mishearing of the lines 'Let me drown in your laughter/Let me die in your arms' transforms a cloying ballad into a suicide pact which given that the song is such sentimental claptrap is a gratifying subversion of it.

John Denver, 'Annie's Song'

 If he was in the US no one would even **batter an eyelid** at what he says because they are all like that over there.

An easy phrase to mishear but one that is rewarding in this form. 'To bat an eyelid' is a useful idiom usually used in the negative – I didn't bat an eyelid; but, misheard, we get a deep-fried, crispy starter of an altogether unsavoury kind. This quote is taken from a chat room on a truly terrifying website called Aussie Pythons and Snakes which is apparently 'Australia's premier online herpetological community'. If they want to batter eyelids, that's fine by me.

www.aussiepythons.com

Eggcorn   Malapropism   Mondegreen

Give me the **Beach Boys** and free my soul.

This misheard line from the 1973 Dobie Gray classic (the *only* Dobie Gray 'classic'?) 'Drift Away' is a definite improvement on the rather bland original, 'Give me the beat boys…'. At the same time as the single came out, the Beach Boys recorded *Holland Album* (an inspired title given it was recorded in the Netherlands) but Brian Wilson's contribution was negligible – allegedly he spent most of the time lying on the floor of his rented house freeing his soul.

Dobie Gray, 'Drift Away'

You don't have to say you love me just **because I'm mad**.

Now there's an ultimatum from Dusty Springfield which has the menacing overtones of Glenn Close and boiled bunnies. What Dusty Springfield actually said was 'just be close at hand'. She had a hit with this in 1966 and it was one of her defining songs. Elvis Presley also used to sing it – he first released it back in the late 50s before any hint of being unhinged was apparent.

Dusty Springfield, 'You Don't Have to Say You Love Me'

Do you need a secretary at your **beckoned call**?

An example of a phrase ('beck and call') in which a word which is no longer used ('beck') is transformed into a word which is immediately recognisable ('beckoned'). 'Beck' in 'beck and call' comes from a shortening (a long time ago) of the verb 'beckon' and came to mean a slight hand gesture expressing a command and then, by extension, a gesture which was immediately obeyed. This last sense and the shortened word are no longer common except in 'beck and call'; hence the use of 'beckoned' which of course takes the phrase back to its roots.

www.worldslist.com

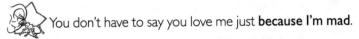 Eggcorn   Malapropism   Mondegreen

crops

 Waste of time. They're all a load of **belladonnas**.

Lord 'Billy' Blyton is said to have uttered this when talking about his colleagues' performance after the first televised debate from the House of Lords. The slip of the tongue from this reportedly affable and unpretentious Labour peer does nothing to dispel the view of many that politics is a poisonous business – and indeed that the malapropism might not also be applied to many modern 'prima donnas'.

 One Sunday after church, Benjamin, 9, asked his mother, 'Will we have to tie the **biblical cord**?' 'No,' my daughter responded, 'Misty will take care of that herself. By the way, Ben, we call it an umbilical cord.' 'Oh,' he said. 'An **unbiblical cord**?'

The joy of malapropisms is that they have no shame or pious inhibitions. Children are particularly adept at repeating to you what they hear or mishear and are equally determined that what they heard is correct. The *biblical cord* it is then.

The *Lutheran*

 Bill Oddie, Bill Oddie, put your hands all over my body.

Bill Oddie may not have been lablled a sex icon before but in some people's ears he is Madonna's man of choice in her 1992 single 'Erotica'. She actually sang 'Erotic' twice but I've got to confess that the image of her exhorting the famous twitcher to get familiar is satisfyingly absurd.

Madonna, 'Erotica'

 He doesn't have the necessary **biro**.

Jonathan Coe's anti-Thatcher novel *What a Carve Up* has one outstanding moment of eggcornery: the hero, Michael Owen, dictates a book review over the phone to his newspaper. Instead of printing his sentence which claimed that the author of the book he is reviewing did

 Eggcorn   Malapropism   Mondegreen

not have 'the necessary brio', the accusation is translated into the rather more mundane 'the necessary biro'. Owen is sacked for someone else's mishearing but the phrase 'necessary biro' works for me. I can think of a number of modern novelists who lack precisely that.

Jonathan Coe, *What a Carve-Up*

 We don't need no **birth control, The dark's a hazard** in the classroom.

See 'Dukes of Hazzard' for a full commentary on one of the 1970s' musical low points (the concept album to end all concept albums – Pink Floyd's *The Wall*). Instead of hearing 'the Floyd's' central message ('We don't need no thought control'), some hear this rather more exciting (but still very significant) proposition. No birth control at school – whatever are they teaching them? Doubly dangerous of course if the lights are turned out.

Pink Floyd, 'Another Brick in the Wall, Part II'

 The articles get **boggled** down in tons of advertising and the layouts usually don't appeal to me. But mainly it's the advertising that bothers me a lot.

The oldest sense of 'boggle' is to fumble or bungle but other slightly later examples show that it has also meant to take fright or be startled which adds another layer of meaning to the original 'bogged down'. So, if you get boggled down in something, there is a distinctly 'Friday the 13th' edge to it all and that makes for a much more exciting kind of problem.

photography-on-the.net

 I guess I'm gonna fade into **Bolivian.**

When asked what the future held for him, Mike Tyson's assertion that the Hand of Fate was going to gently erase him in Bolivia caused a minor flurry of excitement in that part of the world. That is, until they realised that he had been setting about the English language in the same devastating manner as he did his opponents.

 Eggcorn   Malapropism   Mondegreen

Republicans understand the importance of **bondage** between a mother and child.

It seems incredible now but Dan Quayle was once Vice-President of the USA. The man who famously could not spell 'potato' was always suspected of being IQ-lite. His chequered political career came to an end when he finished eighth in the first Primary to secure the Republican nomination for President in 1999. Quayle's focus (and where he caused most controversy) was on family values. He was highly critical of the television series *Murphy Brown* which he perceived to be advocating single-parenthood. His family-values howler here is an example of his ability to shoot himself in the foot.

 She's described in reports as a **bowl** in a china shop.

It is heartening when a tired old cliché ('a bull in a china shop') is mistakenly transformed into a head-scratcher of a phrase. If you are a bowl in a china shop, presumably you are somewhat unremarkable – just a piece of crockery in a safe environment. Safe, that is, until a snorting, ground-pawing cliché comes crashing in. So, 'a *bowl* in a china-shop' enters the language for something unremarkable, normal, safe and secure.

CNN

Listen to the rhythm of the gentle **boxing gopher.**

Petula Clark's classic 1964 single 'Downtown' changes from an exhortation to appreciate a Brazilian dance (the Bossanova) to an appeal to check out a television puppet's pugilism – for to people of a certain generation there is only one famous gopher. Having encountered this mishearing, I can't now listen to it without thinking of Philip Schofield and Gordon the Gopher going ten rounds; the only thing that compensates for that image intruding into my mind is that Gordon always wins.

Petula Clark, 'Downtown'

 Eggcorn   Malapropism   Mondegreen

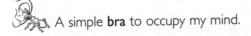 A simple **bra** to occupy my mind.

There aren't many words in REM's 'The One I Love' but this mishearing adds a schoolboy edge to the song. Stipe sings in fact that each 'one' is a 'simple prop' to while away the hours with.

REM, 'The One I love'

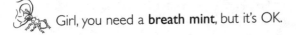 Girl, you need a **breath mint**, but it's OK.

As with KEVIN below, the Backstreet Boys' success with women is not going to be something to shout about if you look at the mondegreens that their songs inspire. This one, again, does not hold out the promise of a long and happy relationship but at least I suppose he is being honest. In fact the lyric is 'girl you leave me breathless, but it's OK' which is about as dull as you can get.

Backstreet Boys, 'Drowning'

 Deck the halls with **Buddy Holly**.

If Christmas seems over-commercialised now, imagine what parents thought in the 1950s when their children misheard the traditional carol 'Deck the halls' and had their favourite pop star replace the more seasonal 'boughs of holly'. Signs indeed that the Victorian Christmas was being ramraided by popular culture. Spare a thought, too, for Charles Hardin Holley, strung up in every home in the land. Oh boy. (See also CHRISTMAS BOX.)

Eggcorn   Malapropism   Mondegreen

GEORGE W. BUSH
The twenty-first century language mangler

Rarely can there have been such an important position filled by one who has such a skewed tongue. 'Dubya' has attained a status among language observers that very few others have managed: in a few short years he has created a category of linguistic incompetence (and in some cases, creativity) all of his own. Collecting Bushisms now provides some journalists with a good living. The Great Gaffer himself is aware of his stumbling reputation but has also said without a hint of irony: 'Anybody who is in a position to serve this country ought to understand the consequences of words.' So please do not misunderestimate him. Here are some that fit the bill as far as this book is concerned:

A tax cut is really one of the **anecdotes** to coming out of an economic illness.

Anyone who thought that George Dubya's grasp of economic theory is tenuous but that perhaps he's not that bothered about it, go to the top of the class. In this statement in 2000, W. shows his economic credentials by mangling 'antidotes' and 'anecdotes'. See also ANTIDOTES.

I am a person who recognises the **fallacy** of humans.

The OED defines 'fallacy' as 'a delusive notion, an error', which is a pretty good description of most of Bush's thought processes by the looks of it. 'Frailty'/'fallacy' – what's the difference to mankind?

Eggcorn   Malapropism   Mondegreen

> I thought how proud I am to be standing up beside my dad. Never did it occur to me that he would become the **gist** for cartoonists.

Dubya defending his dad which, if you're Bush senior, must be as welcome as having Daffy Duck as your lawyer. 'Grist' is the substance or main part of the matter being discussed; 'grist' is literally the corn which is to be ground in a mill and hence that which brings income or profit and probably what W. had in mind.

> We cannot let terrorists and rogue nations hold this nation **hostile** or hold our allies **hostile**.

Being held hostile once is unfortunate, but being held hostile twice is simply careless. George gets his hostages in a twist in the 2000 Presidential campaign.

> I mean, there needs to be a wholesale effort against racial profiling, which is **illiterate** children.

Or indeed, leaders of the US. There should also be a wholesale effort against illegitimate presidents – or did I mean illiterate?

> It's going to require numerous **IRA** agents.

As a faux pas this ranks pretty highly. Bush, I think, meant IRS (Internal Revenue Service) agents but to bring in the IRA to manage tax avoidance is a drastic measure to take to rescue the domestic economy. Still, perhaps the US tax authorities are going to try to help the Northern Ireland peace process.

 Eggcorn   Malapropism   Mondegreen

'This is still a dangerous world,' he told more than 2,000 supporters at an oyster roast. 'It's a world of madmen and uncertainty and potential **mential** losses.'

I included this because it's a new word and I haven't a clue what it means. Answers please to 1600 Pennsylvania Avenue NW, Washington, USA. Even if he meant to say 'mental' it is entirely unclear what he was trying to say.

They said, 'You know, this issue doesn't seem to **resignate** with the people.' And I said, 'You know something? Whether it resignates or not doesn't matter to me, because I stand for doing what's the right thing ...'.

The question is whether to resignate is the right thing to do; many have suggested it as a course of action to cure the US of the blight of Bush: that surely would resonate.

If the **terriers and bariffs** are torn down, this economy will grow,

A straightforward reverse of initial letters but accomplished with such style. There is a certain poetry to the 'terriers' and 'bariffs' that has to be admired.

'The hardest job in America is to be a single mom, making $20,000 a year,' Bush declared at a recent Rotary Club lunch where he promised that as President, he would reduce the struggling woman's marginal income-tax rate and 'knock down her **tollbooth** to the middle class'.

Another instance where the intended meaning is just about clear but the words he uses to convey the meaning really fail to resignate with me.

🐜 Eggcorn   🐜 Malapropism   🐜 Mondegreen

> ... [I'm against] 'hard quotas, quotas that basically delineate based on whatever. However, they delineate, quotas, I think, **vulcanise** society'.

Dubya made this statement when he was still Governor of Texas. When he made it everyone assumed that he meant Balkanise – meaning to divide into small mutually hostile groups – which would have made sense in the context. However, a few days later, the periodical in which the statement was printed issued a clarification indicating that Bush had said 'Balkanise'; we will never know if he meant that quotas improve the strength of rubber or whether he meant that they divide society into smaller hostile groups. Perhaps, like the advice offered by Richard Daley's press secretary (see ASPARAGUS), the magazine should have printed what he meant rather than what he said. Trouble is in George's case you never can quite tell.

> I hear there's rumours on the **Internets** that we're going to have a draft.

Terrifying that a man in control of the most sophisticated technology the world has ever seen should be so clueless when it comes to the Interweb (or so some have had him call it). Bush famously extolled the virtues of 'the Google' when he was asked in a television interview whether he had ever used it. He answered (not entirely to the point) that he liked to pull up the program that showed maps so that he could look at his ranch. It was touchingly simple given that he is also in control of the most sophisticated spying and surveillance network the world has ever seen and uses 'the Google' to have a peek at his home.

> And there is distrust in Washington. I am surprised, frankly, at the amount of distrust that exists in this town. And I'm sorry it's the case, and I'll work hard to try to **elevate** it.

Truth will out.

🐜 Eggcorn　　🪴 Malapropism　　🦗 Mondegreen

Too bad I know **buttkiss** about BIOS editing. You should post a 'how to' thread sometime.

A new development of a truly great word, 'bubkes' (sometimes 'bupkes' or 'bupkus') is probably derived from the Yiddish word *kozebubkes* which means 'goat droppings'. If you know bubkes about something you're as ignorant as it's possible to be on the subject. Fast forward a few decades and enter 'I know buttkiss'. It's tempting to imagine that the new development is 'bubkes' with attitude – roughly translated as 'I know nothing but kiss my butt if I care about that'. There again it could just be that 'buttkiss' was the nearest recognisable word to grab hold of.

www.hardforum.com

 Eggcorn   Malapropism   Mondegreen

BUSH'S ARMY: Hoist by his own **canard**.

Truly a phrase of human ingenuity, 'hoist by his own canard' is a linguistic shrine to give thanks at. The original expression comes from Hamlet:

> Let it work;
> For 'tis the sport to have the enginer
> Hoist with his own petar; and 't shall go hard
> But I will delve one yard below their mines
> And blow them at the moon: O, 'tis most sweet,
> When in one line two crafts directly meet.

where Hamlet plots to alter a letter he suspects to contain his own death warrant to be the death warrant of his travelling companions, Rosencrantz and Guildenstern. 'Hoist with his own petar' simply means blown up by your own bomb. A 'canard', though, is an absurd story or a hoax (as well as being French for 'duck'). So when you mangle 'hoist by his own petard' and 'canard' you get a hoax which comes back to expose the hoaxer. Or, if you want to go for the surreal option, you are strung up by your own duck which takes us into Gary Larson territory. A marvel of linguistic invention and an expression to be used as often as the circumstances allow.

But well I woot thou doost myn herte to erme,/That I almoost have caught a **cardynacle**.

In the Introduction to 'The Pardoner's Tale' in the *Canterbury Tales*, the host Harry Bailey uncertainly lists a number of medical tools and implements and realises that he may have got the words wrong. His comment above means that he is so sad (at the tale that has been told) that he almost had a heart attack. Except he doesn't say heart attack, he mangles the unfamiliar 'cardiacle' (from a Latin word meaning heartburn) and the more commonly used 'cardinal'. This is one of the first malapropisms that we have written down in English.

Chaucer, *The Canterbury Tales*

 Someday you will find me/**Carpeting** the landslide.

This is an excellent mishearing – the image of the Brothers Gallagher out there with the twisted pile trying to cover a freshly fallen heap of rocks is irresistible. It shows that a good mondegreen doesn't have to be a mishearing of a complete line – sometimes just getting one or two words wrong (in this case 'caught beneath') can paint a whole new and funny picture.

Oasis, 'Champagne Supernova'

 **Carpool Tunnel** syndrome.

The carpal tunnel is a narrow rigid passageway made of ligament and bones at the base of the hand. Through it travels the median nerve which controls sensations to the palm side of the thumb and fingers. Problems with it became more prevalent with the increased use of keyboards in office jobs in the 1990s. Carpool Tunnel syndrome is, of course, something entirely different and it provokes some great images of co-workers on their way to the office having paranoid attacks in the dark of the tunnel their car is travelling through. It has all the makings of a vintage Gary Larson cartoon. It has incidentally also been used as a title for a book about extreme parental anxiety.

Eggcorn　　Malapropism　　Mondegreen

And then he [Mike Tyson] will have only **channel** vision.

Mike Tyson's boxing career was distinctive for the raw aggression he displayed in the ring; he had a singular intensity which he directed wholly and very intimidatingly at his opponent. Frank Bruno's description of him only having 'channel vision', I'm afraid, blurs that picture – channel vision is to me more flicking through the stations on the television than single-mindedly beating your opponent to a standstill.

Swing low, sweet **cherry yacht**, **common law** is taking me home.

There has to be a campaign to get this adopted by whatever the rugby equivalent of the Barmy Army is. The original lyrics to this traditional black slave song are 'sweet chariot, coming for to carry me home' but over the course of too many England rugby matches they have dulled. Time for a change: what could be better to breathe new life into the song than a striking cherry-red yacht and the prospect of your partner (very modern) carrying you home after a hard rugby match. Surely more inspiring than a 'sweet chariot' (whatever that is).

'Swing Low, Sweet Chariot'

Thank you for coming home/ Sorry about the **cheese** on the walls.

Like other bands who inspire mishearings, Spandau Ballet's lyrics are often obscure to the point of incomprehensibility. To be frank, Tony Hadley may as well have apologised for the cheese on the walls; it makes as much sense as apologising for the fact that 'the chairs are all worn' which is apparently how the lyrics actually read. (See also FOOD BOX p.62)

Spandau Ballet, 'Gold'

Eggcorn   Malapropism   Mondegreen

The Houston Oilers have left me utterly **chestfallen.**

When a coach creates an image that so aptly describes his broken spirit, you have to admire the way his mind works. Bill Peterson's team has just been hammered, not just beaten, but utterly destroyed and his creative impulses override the disappointment so he can depict how absolutely the defeat has affected him.

Well, that was a **cliff-dweller**.

Like the coach who was utterly 'chestfallen' above, Wes Westrum, a US baseball player and manager, has come up with a whole new mental image to describe sporting emotions. If, previously, during a tense match you'd felt on the edge of your seat or, worse, hanging on to the top of a cliff by your fingernails, imagine now instead being part of a peaceful camp scene on the side of a cliff as the smoke wafts gently into the big blue sky. How much better for the blood pressure to be in that state of mind during a tense game.

I can see **Cleveland now, Lorraine** has gone.

To mishear one word in a lyric, to borrow from Oscar Wilde, is unfortunate; to mishear two is just carelessness. The opening line of Johnny Nash's classic 'I Can See Clearly Now' boasts a rare double: not only is the song title misheard but the opening lines are too. It is also a great example of what I've called 'The Lorraine Syndrome'. (See box on page 93.) So what does it all mean? Is Lorraine a woman with a fuller figure – so much so she blots a whole US city from the landscape? Or did she forbid the singer his abiding wish to visit Cleveland, Ohio and only now that Lorraine has left him can he fulfil his dream? The song is high up in my mondegreen chart because there are mishearings of the second line as well. So, apparently Nash then sings, 'I can see all **lobster claws** in my way'. Whether this is now switching to a fishing nightmare is a matter for separate debate. Nash actually sang 'I can see clearly now the rain has gone/ I can see all obstacles in my way'.

Johnny Nash, 'I Can See Clearly Now'

Eggcorn   Malapropism   Mondegreen

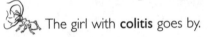 I can't **climb this ceiling** any more.

A dreadful dirge to all but the limpest soft-rock fan, 'I Can't Fight This Feeling Any More' is one of those songs that is a station-changer: guaranteed to make me reach for the presets. If some listeners substitute words about a desperate but failed escape attempt for the song's title, then clearly the song is doing serious psychological damage elsewhere too. Happily, it reached only number 16 in the UK charts in 1984; unhappily, radio stations seem unable to jettison it from their playlists.

REO Speedwagon, 'I Can't Fight this Feeling'

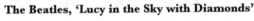 The girl with **colitis** goes by.

An unromantic and unsettling image for someone who might well have just taken vision-enhancing substances. This very famous mondegreen sticks because it contrasts with the dreamy (am I allowed to say trippy?) tone of the song. Colitis is not something that you associate with the glamour world of psychedelic music in the 60s. Mind you, which would you rather have – a curable inflammation or 'kaleidoscope eyes'?

The Beatles, 'Lucy in the Sky with Diamonds'

 It's an old premise that you can't prove a negative in the absence of independent **collaborating** evidence.

Most defence barristers and police officers would give their right arms for the kind of evidence that works together to establish a coherent case. The judge however might be suspicious if the evidence decided to collaborate; he or she would be happier if there was 'corroborating' evidence.

 I've gotta **consecrate** myself on this newspaper.

The ability of *All in the Family* character Archie Bunker to mangle the language is up there with the patron saint of it all, Mrs Malaprop. This fine example would delight most newspaper editors who would like to think that the whole population sat down and consecrated itself on their paper every morning. Happily for the rest of us we don't have to.

 Eggcorn   Malapropism   Mondegreen

CHRISTMAS

After you've decked the halls with 'Buddy Holly', gather round the piano and try singing some of these old favourites:

Nowell, Nowell, Nowell, Nowell, **Barney's** *the King of Israel.* And Fred Flintstone is very cross ... ('Nowell, Nowell, Nowell, Nowell, born is the King of Israel', from 'The First Nowell')

You'll go down and **hit the tree**. Will Rudolph be calling 'Claims Direct'? ('You'll go down in history', from 'Rudolph the Red-nosed Reindeer')

Get dressed ye married *gentlemen*. Speaks for itself. ('God rest ye merry gentlemen', from 'God Rest Ye Merry Gentlemen')

Good King Wences' **car backed out** *on the* **feet of heathen**. Which in my book makes the epithet 'good' very debatable. ('Good King Wenceslas looked out on the feast of Stephen', 'Good King Wenceslas')

We three kings of **porridge and tar**. Doesn't say much for their subjects or their dominions. ('We three Kings of Orient are', from 'We Three Kings')

To hear **slave elves** *in the snow*. Anyone familiar with Hermione Granger's campaign to free the house elves in the Harry Potter books will cringe to hear that there are such things as slave elves... ('To hear sleigh bells in the snow', from '(I'm Dreaming of a) White Christmas')

You will get a **set of metal earrings** / *in your ear*. Which may be preferable to 'sentimental feelings'. ('You will get a sentimental feeling/when you hear', from 'Rockin' Around the Christmas Tree')

Eggcorn   Malapropism   Mondegreen

Olive *the other reindeer used to laugh and call him names.* A humdrum name for the exotic flying deer. ('All of the other reindeer used to laugh and call him names', from 'Rudolph the Red-nosed Reindeer')

The little Lord Jesus laid down his sweet ***ted***. Very sweet. ('The little Lord Jesus laid down his sweet head', from 'Away in a Manger')

Holy ***imbecile***, *tender and mild.* You don't have to be bright to be a religious icon. ('Holy infant, so tender and mild', from 'Silent Night')

Deck the halls with ***bowels of Holly***. A variation on Buddy Holly and a rather gruesome one at that. ('Deck the halls with boughs of holly', from 'Deck the Halls')

Finally, how about this for not quite entering into the spirit of things?

*Peace on earth and mercy mild/****Goddamn*** *sinners reconciled.* ('Peace on earth and mercy mild/God and sinners reconciled', from 'Hark! The Herald Angel Sings')

 Best to carry it openly, then it don't look **conspicious.**

In the first ever episode of *Only Fools and Horses*, Trigger sells Del some dodgy briefcases and advises him that if he's going to walk around with a sample of the merchandise he does so openly. 'Conspicious' works brilliantly not only for the play on 'suspicious' but because he uses 'con' as the prefix which makes the whole deal even more shady than if he'd used the right word.

Trigger, 'Big Brother Del'

Eggcorn   Malapropism   Mondegreen

With the lights out, we're **contagious**.

Surprisingly, although there are lots of cited examples of Nirvana mondegreens, very few of them are any good. Many people mishear one or two words but they do not change greatly the meaning in the song. This one at least suggests a different story – what happens when the lights are on? Everybody better? The actual lyric is 'With the lights out, we're less dangerous'.

Nirvana, 'Smells Like Teen Spirit'

 His whole demeanour has changed from an angry pout to a smiling **continence**.

While we may look for an open, happy countenance, this mishearing gives us a man manically grinning with relief as he manages to uncross his legs and regain control.

 I wan' all dem kids to do what I do, to look up to me. I wan' all the kids to **copulate** me.

Andre Dawson, a Chicago Cubs American football player, mixes together copy and imitate here to lead to a probable jail sentence.

Incredulously, Kepa Blanco scores with his first touch in English football, **coverting** Bobby Zamora's cross from a suspiciously offside-looking position.

Leaving aside that Kepa Blanco must have had his jaw open with incredulity as he scored, this BBC football commentary also mangles the verb 'convert' to create a new possibility: to score covertly or in secret. As if the scorer appeared out of thin air and popped the ball in the net. That really would be worth something to any team.

BBC 5 Live web commentary

 Eggcorn   Malapropism   Mondegreen

We will be revisiting this topic shortly, as it is the **crutch** of the matter.

An eggcorn out of the 'replace obscure words with something recognisable' camp. The 'crux of the matter' refers to the crux as something that torments or troubles (derived from one meaning of 'crucify' – to torment or afflict with great pain) and is therefore something that needs to be solved or removed. Later it was taken up by writers as a means of expressing a conundrum or riddle. It is not used now except in that one expression and so we look for alternatives. 'Crutch' works because it is a support and therefore vital to something being stable.

Financial Sense

She called the turnout at the clinic 'just awesome', but added, 'It's still disturbing to see the cars pulling in ... It just **curdles** my hair'.

There are some mental pictures that produce a physical shudder. This example from an American newspaper is one of them. To imagine your hair changed into a soft, solid mass of curd is to feel a shiver of disgust run down your spine. Blood is often curdled in horror; toes and hair more usually *curl* with embarrassment or fright. Hair-curdling is more unpleasant than either of them.

Dr Sohrab Shahabi and Mr Orhan Isik, Deputy Secretaries General, Economic Cooperation Organisation (ECO) paid a **curtsey call** on the President of the Kyrgyz Republic HE Mr Askar Akaev, on December 21, during his official visit to the Islamic Republic of Iran.

The film of the Deputy Secretaries of the General of Economic Cooperation Organisation bobbing down while holding the pleats of their trousers in respect to the President of the Kyrgyz Republic would be worth seeing. But 'curtsy call' really is in fact a variant of 'courtesy' so from a linguistic point of view it is acceptable.

🌱 Eggcorn   🌿 Malapropism   🐜 Mondegreen

In some communities, agencies get a complaint and the officers who do not have the training to handle it say well, you just need to try a different piece of software or turn off the computer, or if the person who is **cyber-stocking** you meets you face to face, then well you have to deal with it at that point.

Cyberstalking was first legislated against in 1999 in California since when the crime has clearly developed. So, presumably, someone who is guilty of 'cyberstocking' (as in this magazine article) has over-furnished themselves with 'cybers' which compared with defaming someone or victimising them through the Internet seems to me to be a minor crime. Another use of 'cyberstocking' which is gradually emerging is that of the 'sock' you place beneath the electronic chimney to have an online Christmas.

www.govtech.net

🌱 Eggcorn   🍍 Malapropism   🐛 Mondegreen

Dd

I imagine the excitement will last for another few weeks before it peters out into the **damp squid** that faced the party before Bas' well-timed theatrics.

Squid are damp; of that, there can be no doubt. Often, they are wet. Rarely, though, do they perform at parties. The abused word in this newspaper article is 'squib' which means a small (and usually disappointing) firework. When the squib is damp, it falls below even the most meagre of expectations. I imagine that a squid performing at a party might well be a 'damp squib' but it is unlikely we'll ever find out.

Trinidad & Tobago Express

What gets his **dandruff** up is the film 'Loose Change'.

The origins of the phrase 'get your dander up' are pretty obscure. In the late eighteenth century, dander was another word for yeast or the raising agent used to make bread. There is speculation that 'getting your dander up' as an idiom comes therefore from the idea of fermenting – relating the action of fermenting with your temper. For all that, it is now a reasonably obscure phrase and when people reach for it, it is understandable that they look for a recognisable image to associate with it. How this blogger got to 'dandruff' is another matter: perhaps because it is associated with hair and therefore with having your hair stand on end is something only they can answer. Personally I wouldn't like to be facing someone with either their dander or their dandruff up.

 I shot the sheriff but I didn't shoot him **dead you see**.

Let's face it, as a plea for leniency this doesn't really work but it is an improvement on the original. If Clapton's admission was the murder of a sheriff but not the deputy, this mishearing is admitting only attempted murder. Well, that's all right then.

Eric Clapton, 'I Shot the Sheriff'

 This would involve providing a **dedicated** car park for daily parking only.

I've heard of car worship but never car park worship; this excellent recent example of the art of the malaprop conjures the image of a bishop consecrating the hallowed parking bays (for daily worship only?) while commuters and shoppers say their 'Hail Mercedes' before locking the cars. Strictly speaking the university in question should provide a 'designated' car park.

University of Dundee website

 This coverage provides for protection from claims for libel, slander and **deformation** of character.

This nice tweak to 'defamation' from a catering magazine adds a physical edge to 'libel' and 'slander' – to have one's character deformed can only lead to a custodial sentence for the offender, surely?

***Catering* Magazine**

 And yes, if you have clicked the link and downloaded and run it, you have been infected by a virus … But **deserves** you right for not seeing how fake the whole thing is.

This is a great example of a word on the cusp on becoming mainstream. The fact that someone 'deserves' something means that

Eggcorn   Malapropism   Mondegreen

instead of it 'serving them right' when they lay themselves open to a problem, it 'deserves them right' to find themselves in that particular pickle. Watch how this phrase becomes more and more mainstream over the coming years.

 This leads me to believe the City of Toledo is a fan of cutting off its nose **despite** its face.

Some eggcorns inadvertently take us back to a word's origins. This is one such case: 'spite' is actually the shortened form of 'despite' which as a verb used to mean to express contempt for something. So 'to spite' and 'to despite' are synonymous. I can see on the horizon more and more cases where 'despite' on its own replaces 'to spite', particularly in this one phrase.

 It's a proven fact that Capital Punishment is a **detergent** for crime.

Hanging kills all known germs … dead. A debatable point but if soap powder makes criminals think twice before offending then so be it. This excellent example of the gift of the gaffe first appeared on the US sitcom *All in the Family*, since when it has spread. I haven't yet heard anyone mention nuclear detergent though – now, that would be a powerful cleaner.

All in the Family

Diarrhoea/ Here I go again.

My, my, how can I resist you? A really, really bad mishearing which does cast the song 'Mamma Mia' into a completely different light. 'Diarrhoea, does it show again?' and so it goes on. A meditation on the stubbornness of Montezuma's Revenge or a song about a boyfriend who, for all his faults, is irresistible? See also PORTALOO.

Abba, 'Mamma Mia'

Eggcorn   Malapropism   Mondegreen

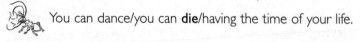 You can dance/you can **die**/having the time of your life.

Abba had an excellent command of English. They were also, on the whole, optimists. Why, then, would anyone mishear 'jive' and replace it with 'die'? It happened with the result that the best time of your life seems to be when you're dead. A truly absurd notion. That is, if your ears receive a glancing blow from an Abba song.

Another phrase from the song, where the band exhort you to take the rhythm from the tambourine, has also had various re-interpretations, the best of which is 'eat a bean off a tambourine', which strikes me as a very difficult instruction for someone dancing.

Abba, 'Dancing Queen'

 I don't want no other love, baby/ It's just you I'm **diggin'** up.

Elvis's song 'Don't Be Cruel' has to my mind always been about a man hopelessly in love pining for the love of his life to 'at least please telephone' and say 'I do'. For others the story is more tragic: his love has died and he, inconsolable at her loss, is about to commit a terrible crime in the Burke and Hare line. In fact, he actually said 'It's just you I'm thinkin' of '.

Elvis Presley, 'Don't Be Cruel'

I've got a bad case of **dire rear**.

Or, indeed, gross INCONTINENCE. Eggcorns can help in all sorts of ways: often the misheard word is more modern and fits the occasion better than the original word. In this case, the eggcorn is rather too descriptive of a condition which from its etymology simply means 'a flowing through'. This new description of the physical manifestation of the condition is not to be encouraged.

Eggcorn   Malapropism   Mondegreen

It debunks the attempted propaganda ... to cast **dispersion** against the re-established State of Israel ...

In which case, the attempted propaganda is throwing a scattering of things against its target – perhaps a little like a verbal blunderbuss and therefore a lot less effective than the more usual 'cast aspersions'.

www.christianforums.com

So, you'd be amazed that the number of people that accept opportunities in startups without doing some basic fundamental **do diligence**.

The normal legal phrase for work carried out to establish a companies assets and liabilities (usually prior to a take-over) is 'due diligence' which has been around since the late sixteenth century. In fact, it is perfectly acceptable to use the phrase 'do diligence' but usually only when 'do' is used as a verb. (See also DO PROCESS.)

media.podtech.net

The law says you are innocent till proven guilty; you have to go through do process.

While 'do diligence' is a marginal eggcorn and is included because it is just an odd-sounding phrase when used incorrectly, 'do process' is an example of a new phrase created by taking a current colloquial building block ('We're going to "do" Hollywood', for example), combining it with a very old legal expression (due process). The result is frankly weird. There is perhaps now a 'do process' and a 'don't process'?

 Eggcorn   Malapropism   Mondegreen

DOGBERRYISMS:

(from *Much Ado About Nothing*)

Shakespeare's malapropist

Mrs Malaprop is Constable Dogberry's direct descendant. In *Much Ado About Nothing*, he attempts to use impressive words but mangles the language to the point where Don Pedro remarks of him, 'this learned constable is too cunning to be understood'. He chiefly manages to say exactly the opposite of what he intends.

*You are thought here to be the most **senseless** and fit man for the constable of the watch.* (III.iii.23)

*This is your charge: you shall **comprehend** [apprehend] all **vagrom** [vagrant] men.* (III.iii.25)

*Marry, sir, I would have some **confidence** [conference] with you, that **discerns** [concerns] you nearly.* (III.v.2)

*Our watch, sir, have indeed **comprehended** [apprehended] two **auspicious** [suspicious] persons, and we would have them this morning examined before your worship ... It shall be **suffigance** [sufficient].* (III.v.43)

*Only get the learned writer to set down our **excommunication** [examination].* (III.v.58)

*Thou wilt be condemned into everlasting **redemption** (perdition /damnation) for this.* (IV.ii.58)

*I humbly give you leave to depart, and if a merry meeting may be wished, God **prohibit** (permit) it!* (V.i.314)

The true matter is: it's a **doggy-dog world** out there, and they're all in it for the money.

The phrase 'dog-eat-dog' probably derives from an earlier proverb 'dog does not eat dog' meaning that villains don't turn on each other. If things are really bad then they do and the world become 'dog eat dog'. A 'doggy dog-world' is an altogether safer place where all the inhabitants are small, fluffy and obedient.

Eggcorn · Malapropism · Mondegreen

The bride bless the day, the **dogs say goodnight.**

Louis Armstrong's 1967 single, 'What A Wonderful World' single was a celebration of all that was good in the world as an attempt to take some of the racial and political tension out of the air in the US of the time. While 'trees of green' and 'red roses' were blooming for everyone individually, the image that 'the dogs say good night' is not a happy one as they howl down the moon keeping everyone awake. However, the idea that the bride blesses the day is an apt one for the song – even if it is a mishearing. The original lyrics are 'The bright blessed day, dark sacred nights'.

Louis Armstrong, 'What a Wonderful World'

 That man is a real charmer, a regular **Don Coyote.**

Don Juan with four legs, a bushy tale and a howl that you can hear for miles – the image of the archetypal philanderer will never be the same again.

 Doughnuts make my brown eyes blue.

Crystal Gale does have the most amazing blue eyes and, here, everyone, is the secret: she eats loads of doughnuts. Sadly, though, this is only a great mishearing; no secrets are revealed because the lyric (indeed song title) of this 1977 hit is 'Don't it make my brown eyes blue'.

Crystal Gale, 'Don't It Make My Brown Eyes Blue'

Wrighty was outstanding but the whole team performance, especially the patches when we passed the ball well and moved it about the diamond, was top **draw.**

The phrase 'out of the top drawer' is used figuratively to describe something of the very best quality or the highest level. What something that is out of the 'top draw' might be, as in this post-match interview with Frank Lampard, is open to conjecture: perhaps the best pen and ink depiction of the game?

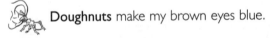 Eggcorn   Malapropism   Mondegreen

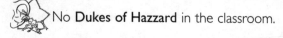 No **Dukes of Hazzard** in the classroom.

When the album *The Wall* came out in 1979, it provoked a sickening spew of adoration. Against the background of the explosion of punk a few years before, the 'concept album' (a phrase to plant terror in any self-respecting teenager's heart) was suddenly centre stage again, and MOR fans were in Heaven; every hi-fi shop in the land belted out songs from the album to show off the sound quality of their systems and liberals lauded the anti-rote-learning 'message'. Nearly thirty years on and the album is firmly rooted in rock history as the concept album to end all concept albums (if only); there are websites devoted to analysis of the songs, the lyrics and the film and the band recently re-formed to perform some of the songs at the London Live 8 Concert. What makes this mishearing particularly satisfying, then, is that in fact 'The Floyd' were lamenting the absence of Bo and Luke Duke from the classroom all along. If the teachers went after them, presumably they just jumped in The General Lee and gunned it out of school. Lucky them. See BIRTH CONTROL for more on 'Another Brick in the Wall'.

Pink Floyd, 'Another Brick in the Wall Part II'

 Either way, it will be a huge help to you in climbing out of the **dull-drums** that occasionally creep up, and start to see huge possibilities for your life.

The doldrums have been a place for those who are down in the dumps since the beginning of the nineteenth century – later in the century, sailors christened a region where their ships were likely to be becalmed the 'equatorial doldrums'; but what are the 'dull-drums' – is it the vague, throbbing headache which makes you feel sluggish and low? There are a load of bad puns waiting to happen here (a lack of timpani for my sorrow?) but 'dull-drums' is a good new way of describing being down in the mouth: an annoying, low-level, background feeling that something isn't right.

womenforwealth.blogspot.com

Eggcorn · Malapropism · Mondegreen

Ee

 Love **Earth**, love **stars**, love **Moon, and Mars.**

'Love Hurts' is a classic which has been recorded by many great singers and bands. One version that doesn't rank particularly highly in my book but which inspired this mondegreen is by Nazareth (Gram Parsons' and Emmylou Harris's version couldn't be misheard in this way) but the universe as a backdrop to the tragedy of unrequited love is appropriate. The actual lyrics are 'Love hurts, love scars, love wounds, it mars'.

Nazareth, 'Love Hurts'

I got so stuck on **eBay**.

Don't we all? Nelly Furtado's 2001 single is generally thought of as a soulful meditation on the way love develops and strengthens; some, though, hear an altogether more prosaic line than the original 'I get so stuck on leaving'. 'Sitting on the dock of eBay' anyone?

Nelly Furtado, 'My Love Grows Deeper'

A stool pile of deerskin, **eggcorns**, and tree bark was also found. A tree with bark stripped from it approximately 8 to 10 feet high was noticed.

The word 'acorn' has had a troubled and disputed path to its current meaning and its spelling has altered much along the way. How appropriate it seems therefore that in the latest twist in its development it should lend its name to a new category of linguistic creation. Eggcorns are generally new words or new expressions which originate from a mishearing of an existing word. At some stage, no doubt, someone will start calling them 'acorns'.

www.lofro.net

TOP TEN EGGCORNS

A personal selection from the book representing the best, most inventive additions to the language. There's a slight cheat here because I have put forward as the winners two words I have put together in the main text of the book simply because they work in the same kind of way.

1 *It has a good climax and some wicked visuals, not really for the* **screamish** *but watchable. It is way more gory than I thought it would be, so if you are* **squirmish** *you may want to skip this one. Beyond that though, it's a really good film.*

2 *It was all hugely entertaining and, one suspects, very much* **thumb in cheek**.

3 *Tourists who come to visit us have the opportunity to enjoy the traditional culture of the region (mixture of Romanian, Greek, Macedonian and Turkish influences) and as well as* **reek the benefits** *of the modern tourist facilities.*

4 *Bush's Army: Hoist by his own* **canard**.

5 *I guess I'm gonna fade into* **Bolivian**.

6 *She called the turnout at the clinic 'just awesome', but added, 'It's still disturbing to see the cars pulling in ... It just* **curdles** *my hair'.*

7 *There is no* **surefool** *way of proceeding.*

8 *A stool pile of deerskin,* **eggcorns**, *and tree bark was also found. A tree with bark stripped from it approximately 8 to 10 feet high was noticed.*

9 *This is my brother's friends* **lipsinging** *'We Are the Champions' by Queen.*

10 **Lack toast** *and intolerant.*

Eggcorn   Malapropism   Mondegreen

I desired to see new things. I desired to experience vol-
umes. And I would be **electrical** to meet an American.

Jonathan Safran Foer creates a master butcher of the English language
called Alex in his novel *Everything Is Illuminated*. Alex acts as a translator
for a man seeking someone who may have saved his grandfather from
the Nazis. The language he uses is part thesaurus abuse and part
malapropism. This is an example of thesaurus abuse. See also FLACCID.

Jonathan Safran Foer, *Everything Is Illuminated*

 Don't ever wear yellow, dear. It makes your skin look
shallow and **emancipated**.

Advice that may have been taken seriously one hundred years ago but
is frowned upon now. Mind you, this website malapropism is an enticing
image of skin freed from the tyranny of the body, having demonstrated
with placards for years to be liberated. Freedom for follicles!

 Cry me a river/ that leads to **erosion**.

Destiny's Child's 2001 remake of the Samantha Sang song
'Emotion' brought physical geography to a whole new generation of
fans – or at least those who heard that rivers cause 'erosion' rather
than leading to 'an ocean'.

Destiny's Child, 'Emotion'

 They [the dead] … have too hastily signed over their
Power of **Eternity**.

Quoted on Jeanette Winterson's blog, this malapropism is truly going
too far. As if it's not bad enough being dead, some have now signed
away their right to be dead forever. A fate worse then death, indeed.

Eggcorn   Malapropism   Mondegreen

We've got hundreds of sites to **exploit**, looking for the chemical and biological weapons that we know Saddam Hussein had prior to our entrance into Iraq.

Malapropisms often reveal what's really going on in the mind of the speaker. George W. selects 'exploit' over 'explore' and, as Del Boy might say, 'fromage frais', he shows you what he is really thinking. Whether the sites were exploited or explored, the chemical and biological weapons appear to have vanished.

 Further, if the applicant/nominee has financial need or **exterminating** circumstances, which could prevent his continued enrolment, a statement describing these circumstances should be attached.

The word 'extenuating' is often only used in the phrase 'extenuating circumstances' so perhaps it is not a surprise when we reach out for a more familiar word. This is a little extreme but fans of *Doctor Who* will be appreciative of the creation of a phrase which could almost have been created for a Dalek plotline.

www.farmhouse.org

 These deals allow cardholders to pay off their credit card debt over a long period of time without accruing more debt due to **exuberant** interest rates.

The thought that interest rates might be having a wild party while all around them sink into a slough of debt and depression is a galling one. However, there is a certain charm in these much-loathed percentages letting their hair down for a while … The writer on this website might have been safer with 'exorbitant'.

cardguide.co.uk

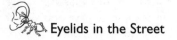 Eyelids in the Street

An outstanding horror movie mishearing of Kenny Rogers and Dolly Parton's 1983 duet 'Islands in the Stream' and appropriately enough it was the first single from Rogers' album *Eyes that See in the Dark*.

Kenny Rogers and Dolly Parton, 'Islands in the Stream'

Eggcorn   Malapropism   Mondegreen

How will the major state political players (both parties) be involved? Is the result a **far gone** conclusion? What side will the major papers take?

The original phrase 'foregone conclusion' is from *Othello* (III.iii.420) where the Moor is responding to Iago's attempt to convince him of Cassio's intentions towards Desdemona.

IAGO: Nay, this was but his dream.

OTHELLO: But this denoted a foregone conclusion.

There are various theories as to the phrase's precise meaning but the general sense of something concluded before it has started or a *fait accompli* is clear. A 'far gone' conclusion however is something that is pretty certain but not absolutely set in stone. A useful eggcorn providing an extra nuance – even if those using it do not intend it so.

This is an exercise in **fertility.**

Which is a different thing altogether from the normal exercise of 'futility'. Perhaps, rather than just enjoying the gaffe, there is a new euphemism here for fertility treatment or indeed 'trying for a baby' – in a rather John Majorish kind of way of course.

Filleted woman ain't got no soul.

'Black Dog' is a raucous song about a singer's desperate desire for love after a failed relationship left him broke. The former love is actually 'big-legged' not 'filleted' although from the tone of the song, you suspect that the singer might prefer the misheard version.

Led Zeppelin, 'Black Dog'

Find this guy and tell this guy and lift your arms to beg this guy/And ask this guy and ask this guy/To fall on me.

REM's 1986 single 'Fall on Me' has been variously interpreted. Two theories seem appropriate here: the first is that it is about oppression in general, and the second that it is about acid rain and its effect on the environment specifically. There is clearly, though, a group of people out there who think that the song is about a desperate manhunt where the chaser ultimately wants to prostrate himself in front of the sought man. What the outcome of this search is we are not told. The actual lyrics are 'Buy the sky and sell the sky and lift your arms up to the sky/And ask the sky and ask the sky/Don't fall on me', but, to be frank, who knows what Michael Stipe is singing about most of the time? Hats off to those who managed to make three coherent lines out of the song.

REM, 'Fall on Me'

 You must be as strong in March, when the **fish** are down.

Not many gaffes by non-native speakers are included in this book because it didn't seem either appropriate or fair to do so. Gianluca Vialli's terrific blunder deserves attention because of this irresistible picture of depressed fish. Vialli explained a few years later that he made the gaffe from a confusion in his own mind for the Italian word for casino chips which apparently translates as 'fish'. Hence the gaffe. Still, 'when the fish are down' is a phrase that warrants general usage.

Eggcorn   Malapropism   Mondegreen

An American in Ukraine is so **flaccid** to recognise.

See ELECTRICAL for more information on Alex, one of the heroes of Safran Foer's novel. This is another example of the thesaurus abuse which he uses to great effect throughout.

Jonathan Safran Foer, *Everything Is Illuminated*

 This Spanish style **flamingo** costume will make you want to dance! **Flamingo** costume includes black and red satin dress, trimmed with black lace, hidden back zipper, clear shoulder straps and rose accessory.

I would have thought that the dress would be pink given the colour of the bird. Often misheard, mis-spoken and misunderstood, 'flamenco' is a word whose etymology no one is sure of. The dance and music came about when at least four different cultures started to blend in Southern Spain in medieval times. An exotic past, to which the picture of the gawky flamingo hardly does justice.

 ## Flies in Outer Space

Billy Idol's 1984 single 'Eyes Without a Face' is a pretty dark tale of a disintegrating love affair. If, as some people do, you hear that flies are in outer space, the next line in the (actual) chorus suggests that 'you got no human grace' which is probably true. However, the abiding image is the scourge of the summer flying around the universe which in the contrast between the vastness of space and the tiny body is an appealing one.

Billy Idol, 'Eyes Without a Face'

Eggcorn   Malapropism   Mondegreen

I then explained that I saw and I have video footage of Jamaicans dressed in African Garms doing a **floorless** display of African dance.

Which is pretty impressive by anyone's standards. Anything described as 'floorless' gets my vote: there are examples of Europeans having 'floorless' English accents, football teams playing 'floorless' football and someone performing 'floorless' manoeuvres to achieve her black belt in karate which really is something out of *Crouching Tiger, Hidden Dragon*. It can only be a matter of time before both 'floorless' and 'floored' creep like ivy over the words 'flawless' and 'flawed'.

www.blackchat.co.uk

 Each student is expected to spread the word at home, and eventually – the hope is – new attitudes will spread like **wild flowers** across Cambodia.

Perhaps a coinage of the peace-loving 60s, this much less threatening alternative to 'wild fire' has a gentle, 'blowing in the wind' feel which makes it entirely appropriate for this book.

www.dfire.org

 We name our **fondlings** in alphabetical order.

Thus Mr Bumble, the beadle in *Oliver Twist*. The way the orphans are treated of course is anything but 'fondly' but the cruel beadle is admired for his sophisticated command of English by those around him even though his comic malapropisms demonstrate his pomposity to the reader.

Charles Dickens, *Oliver Twist*

🌱 Eggcorn   🌿 Malapropism   🐝 Mondegreen

I'm more than a man who **fornicates sheep**.

Superman gets his chance to say what it's like being a superhero in Five for Fighting's 2001 hit. Given this chance, you'd have thought he'd concentrate on his attractive, heroic qualities. Clearly not according to some listeners who hear him making some pretty disgusting admissions and in the process setting the expectations bar pretty low. The original line is 'I'm more than a man in a funny red sheet' which, come to think of it, isn't much of a claim is it? (See also OLD AND HAIRY.)

Five for Fighting, 'Superman (It's Not Easy)'

French benefits.

The attractions of 'French benefits' as opposed to the mundane 'fringe' ones are legion. Folding a number of French traditions and products (a decent lunch break, for example) into your work 'package' would be a temptation too great to resist. This eggcorn first came to light in a FedEx advert and prompted much comment. Sadly, I haven't been able to find any genuine (ab)uses of it but it's too good an expression to let go.

You've got mud on your face, **front disc brakes**.

The only rival REM have for the honour 'Most Misheard Band' is Queen. Even anthems such as this are prone to mishearings which is a tribute to Freddie Mercury's diction (and sometimes the obscurity of the lyrics; see entries from 'Bohemian Rhapsody' and 'Killer Queen'). Instead of 'a big disgrace' some invoke Freddie's penchant for vehicles from the earlier 'I Want to Ride My Bicycle' and move it up a level to a car.

Queen, 'We Will Rock You'

FOOD

We live in consumerist times and it seems logical that lots of songs take on a new life when food intrudes into otherwise unsuspecting lyrics. 'Cheese' and 'sausages' are far and away the most popular intruders – subverting many profound insights, declarations of love and high-flown metaphors. The result is that songs become a celebration of our everyday foodstuffs – which is no bad thing. Here are just a few examples of food creeping into songs which were not intentionally written for the hungry.

Sweet dreams are made of **cheese**.

Ah, but don't eat it just before you go to bed or the dreams won't be sweet, apparently.

Eurythmics, 'Sweet Dreams (Are Made of This)'

Last night I dreamed of **some bagels**.

It was probably the cheese that did it. 'San Pedro' is the original lyric.

Madonna, 'La Isla Bonita'

No **mayonnaise in** Ireland.

Bad luck that. Joan Baez's call to love fellow man actually used John Donne's line 'No Man is an Island' and Hellman's had nothing to do with it.

Joan Baez, 'No Man is an Island'

It's a **fruit, fruit samba**.

. . . which conjures comfortable images of pineapple rings and melon balls; not teenage angst about 'a cruel, cruel summer'.

Bananarama, 'Cruel Summer'

Eggcorn   Malapropism   Mondegreen

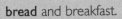 **bread** and breakfast.

A whole new seaside town rip-off – you don't get to sleep but you do get an extra round of white sliced with your full English.

http://www.honeysucklecottages.com.au

gonna use my style/gonna use my **sausage**.

A big ask for the (in)famous vegetarian and animal-rights campaigner Chrissie Hynde. Still a better image than the original 'sidestep'.

The Pretenders, 'Brass in Pocket'

Silence like a **casserole**.

It is axiomatic now that the dead of night is quiet as the casserole, or so some would have us believe; Simon and Garfunkel's haunting simile that 'silence like a cancer grows' has sadly been lost on many listeners who hear with their stomachs.

Simon and Garfunkel, 'The Sound of Silence'

Knee deep in **doughnuts**, children at your feet.

This mondegreen is so far-fetched it had to be included. If you listen to the song, it is pretty clear what the lyric (and indeed title) is. At a push, if you really twist your ears you could mishear 'Lady' as 'knee deep' but mishearing 'Madonna' for 'doughnuts' is a triumph of mondegreening.

The Beatles, 'Lady Madonna'

Eggcorn   Malapropism   Mondegreen

Sparing his life for his mum's **sausages**.

Now, they must be very good. The grammar is a bit obscure here: whose mum's sausages are we talking about – the assailant's or the victim's? It's an important point. The real line in this instance is 'Sparing his life for this monstrosity'. There are other versions of this lyric which makes it a contender for most misheard line. One of the other versions I have come across is 'Spare him his life from this warm sausage tea'.

Queen, 'Bohemian Rhapsody'

A birthday, with **a pot of cheese**.

Cheese fondue anyone? Eva Cassidy's line actually read 'A birthday, with apologies' but 'pot of cheese' seems to me to be as good a way of saying sorry as anything else.

Eva Cassidy, 'Anniversary Song'

Get up in the morning, **baked beans** for breakfast/So that everyone can be fed/Oh, oh, my ears are alight.

The picture of Desmond Dekker giving his poor family individual baked beans for breakfast is a sorry one; luckily his ears are burning with the shame of it all too. In fact, he goes 'slaving for bread, sir'.

Desmond Dekker and the Aces, 'Israelites'

Eggcorn   Malapropism   Mondegreen

 no pain, no **game**.

The economic recession in Britain in the late 1980s and early 1990s led to the then Conservative government raising interest rates to unprecedentedly high levels. The slogan of the time was 'if it isn't hurting, it isn't working' or, in other words, 'no pain, no gain'. A slightly less serious consequence of not suffering before you get your reward is promised in this eggcorn which could be applied to children or sports stars.

 At Roman banquets, the guests wore **garlics** in their hair.

If so, it is amazing that the Empire lasted so long and that the banquets were apparently so debauched. This assertion from a student exam paper takes the 'garland'.

 When he makes a decision, there's no arms thrown into the air, and no **gestating**.

Niall Quinn – leading Ireland goalscorer, manager, racehorse and now football-club owner – was a pundit for a while before he bought Sunderland FC. This comment offered on a Premiership referee was going to be complimentary until some basic ignorance of human biology got in the way.

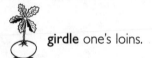 **girdle** one's loins.

Both 'girdle' and the original word in the expression 'gird' are derived from the same Old English *gyrdan*. It's not a huge leap of the imagination therefore to see that in the absence of the word 'gird' in everyday speech, we reach out for the word (albeit not that common) 'girdle' to replace it. The next phase of development of the expression though might well be replacing 'loins' with something more common.

 I'm gonna give you every inch of my **gloves**.

Led Zeppelin's 1969 song from the *Led Zeppelin II* album was adapted for the radio transmission to take out a controversial 'orgasm section' in the middle. Apparently, the station managers felt it was unfit for public airing. There is a suggestion that this mondegreen of the famous line 'I'm gonna give you every inch of my love' is also a sanitised version; or it could be that Robert Plant was feeling particularly generous. The song opens with the line 'You need coolin', baby, I'm not foolin''. But some have heard it again rather more innocently: 'You need **Kool-Aid**/Well maybe I made **Kool-Aid**'. This is a rare example where the innuendo is lost and something altogether more innocent comes out of the mishearing.

Led Zeppelin, 'Whole Lotta Love'

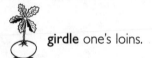 This network is the **goal** standard when it comes to network journalism, television journalism, either domestically or internationally.

The gold standard is the measure against which the value of a nation's currency is assessed. The 'goal' standard is perhaps the measure of a country's footballing prowess and another way of assessing the country's worth. Oh dear.

transcripts.cnn.com

 Eggcorn 　 Malapropism 　 Mondegreen

Our old Toyota just got us through and then gave up the **goat**.

If you give up the ghost, you die; but if you give up the goat the consequences are rather less serious: a switch to cow's milk; renouncing mohair sweaters perhaps or using a lawnmower to keep the grass neat. Nothing life-threatening.

ABC Rural

Then I saw her face, now I'm **gonna leave her**.

In the great tradition of truly macho song lyrics, this ranks very high – had it, of course, actually been the lyric. The Monkees' wonderful song starts by describing a lonely bitter man who can't find love – it 'was meant for someone else but not for me' – who is then transformed into a besotted crooner after experiencing love at first sight – 'Then I saw her face, now I'm a believer'. Some people exhibit a rare and admirable talent to completely ignore this set-up though. For, having been pining for love, this moaning man is turned into a heartless bastard who having found someone promptly dumps her. Worth a top ten slot just for the snappy decision making.

The Monkees, 'I'm a Believer'

I've **got the runs** like a rolling bolt of thunder.

There you are out at a party (late December, back in '63) and someone who you think you might just like walks in. You see her, things are looking promising but you feel a lurch in your stomach (remember there weren't the medications available that there are now) and it ends all way too soon. Your digestion does its imitation of a landslide and your romantic thoughts hit the skids. Frankie Valli the Four Seasons' enduring classic from 1975 was the night that might have been for some listeners: cut short by a storm in the stomach. The original lyrics are 'I felt a rush like a rolling bolt of thunder'.

Frankie Valli & the Four Seasons, December, 1963,
'Oh What a Night'

Eggcorn   Malapropism   Mondegreen

It's hard to realise how much you take something for **granite** until you don't have it. Having a living room in San Francisco has us jumping for joy in appreciation.

If you take something for granted of course, you pay it little heed because you assume it to be true, or you value it too lightly because it is always there or available; so this new sense introduced by mishearing 'granted' works if you assume granite is a common stone of little or no value. However, granite is valued for its durability and strength so the phrase 'take something for granite' could in fact mean that you rely on those characteristics inherent in what you are 'taking'.

nerdsoup.blogspot.com

Please be truthful, but also please be benevolent, please. **Guilelessly**, Alexander.

Jonathan Safran Foer makes great use of his thesaurus again as Alex signs his letter without any guile. See also ELECTRICAL and FLACCID for further examples.

Jonathan Safran Foer, *Everything Is Illuminated*

 Who you gonna call? **Gus Foster**

Not everyone likes the film 'Ghostbusters' but a lot of people loved the theme tune. Written by Ray Parker Jnr and subject to a lawsuit by Huey Lewis (who claimed Parker had ripped off one of his songs – a claim that was settled out of court), it stayed at Number One in 1984 until knocked off by Stevie Wonder no less. The appeal of the mishearing is the need in some people's ears to invent an imaginary (and quite ordinary) person to deal with their supernatural goings-on. I'm sure the film would have done fine if it had been called 'Gus Foster' but perhaps it would have lacked the dramatic punch of 'Ghostbusters'?

Ray Parker Jr, 'Ghostbusters'

Eggcorn   Malapropism   Mondegreen

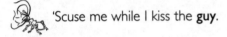 'Scuse me while I kiss the **guy**.

This is one of the most famous mondegreens possibly because it comes from one of Jimi Hendrix's signature songs 'Purple Haze'; possibly also because, on occasion, Hendrix sang the mondegreen rather than the original lyric.

Jimi Hendrix, 'Purple Haze'

Eggcorn   Malapropism   Mondegreen

As long as one invokes the **hack-kneed** platitudes of 'national security' or 'the war on terror', there is virtually no crime that is too extreme.

Apart from chopping someone's knees off? 'Hackneyed' used to mean that something was kept for hire and quickly gained the extra sense of something that had been made dull and uninteresting by overuse. Clichés and platitudes may be irritating but it seems extreme to chop them off at the knees. There is one further use that I can think of for 'hack-kneed' and that is one for football commentators: a forward who has suffered at the hands of a centre-back.

Al-Jazeera

A **half-asked** effort produces **half-asked** results.

I'm not sure you can get more 'am I bovvered' than this. The original US adjective expresses a lack of significance, adequacy or completeness and dates back to the early 1930s. This new take on it (perhaps born out of a desire to avoid the vulgar connotations of 'half-assed') is appropriate for a society that seems to have less and less time to do anything.

Bodybuilding Forum

Helplessly hoping/Her **hard-lickin' lover's** nearby.

The meaning of the Crosby, Stills, Nash and Young song 'Helplessly Hoping' has been much discussed but this mishearing takes it graphically in a very specific direction. That's quite enough of that, I think. The actual lyric is 'Helplessly hoping her harlequin hovers nearby', which is in itself an exercise in pointless alliteration.

Crosby, Stills, Nash and Young, 'Helplessly Hoping'

Not stopping there, Colson states that the multi-faith gathering came within a **hare's breath** of becoming a full-scale prison riot – his ability to quiet the Christian prisoners being the pivotal factor.

A hair's breadth is one of those phrases that demands to be eggcorned; and people have coined a couple of duly alternatives. Quite why this commentator thought that a rabbit's sigh was the appropriate way to describe how close a prison came to rioting is not clear. The other example creates an even more bizarre picture: *Even in this age of fast food and automation, our body's natural balancing mechanism brings us within a **hair's breath** of weight equilibrium.* The body is capable of many remarkable things but I have yet to hear even the battiest therapist talk about letting your hair breathe. The final possibility is a 'hare's breadth' but I haven't yet seen anyone decide that the width of a large rabbit is an apt description for anything.

There's a great **harmonium** in the dressing room.

Sir Alf Ramsey won the World Cup for England in 1966 by being a great tactician and very strict manager. Surprising then that he allowed a huge musical instrument into the dressing room. Pity Sven didn't think of it in 2006 and Steve McClaren seems tone-deaf even at this early stage of his England career.

Eggcorn　　Malapropism　　Mondegreen

Wednesday is country night at the Irish Village. Try your **hat** at country line dancing and country karaoke.

The common phrase for testing whether you have the aptitude at something is 'try your hand' which seems to have first started to be used in the early part of the eighteenth century. Why, though, we now hear people attempting to see whether their hat is up to the task of country line dancing or any manner of other things, is quite baffling. The image though is beguiling – a Stetson bobbling gently up and down, while the caller shouts out the next step is one that sticks with me.

However, nobody seemed concerned about the problems ending the segment sharing stock tips to profit from other people's financial **heartship**.

When times are tough, when you're down to your last few coins and the creditors are knocking on the door, and you are going through financial hardship, how much more poetic if you were experiencing heartship?

www.newshounds.us

It will be interesting to see if the same people that trash other speakers for having less than ruler flat frequency responses will **heave** scorn at these speakers as well.

Normally, we 'heap' scorn on someone and that to me has always seemed enough – both effort and scorn. However, in these excessive times, some clearly feel the expression needs more weight and prefer to 'heave' scorn. Worse, 'heave' also has a euphemistic sense of the 'technicolor yawn'; if you are 'heaving' scorn on someone that is really very unappealing.

🌴 Eggcorn   🍍 Malapropism   🐜 Mondegreen

Heineken remover.

This eggcorn may be more sinned against than sinning, as I haven't been able to establish an absolute bona fide example of it being used. It is, though, a very good alternative to the original 'Heimlich manoeuvre' which is a first-aid technique to help people get rid of something stuck in their throat; a Heineken remover is what you need at the end of a long night in the pub and deserves its place in the First Aid Manual.

This evidence was clearly **heresy** and therefore not admissible to the court.

This is a curious example of an eggcorn where both words 'hearsay' and 'heresy' have been spotted standing in for each other. In this instance, there are overtones of the Spanish Inquisition.

It's a **home** of contention.

The phrase 'bone of contention' is meant to have derived from the phrase 'to cast a bone between two dogs'. In other words, it was an action intended to provoke a fight. In this era of divorce and separation, perhaps the person who mishears 'home' for 'bone' is simply shifting the image to the modern day where two former partners (or their legal representatives) scrap viciously over ownership of the love nest. Failing that it is simply a family which argues a lot.

Show them **hot monkey**.

A mondegreen to tread around very carefully. This is a good example where Michael Jackson's life enters the listener's subconscious and changes the song. While Bubbles's (the singer's monkey) fame has diminished (apparently he is now living on a ranch

 Eggcorn   Malapropism   Mondegreen

somewhere in California), the association of chimp and master is still very strong. The song 'Beat It' is about avoiding fighting and displaying how cool you are by walking away from violence. So, instead of showing your would-be assailant 'how funky' you are, some people believe you have to show 'hot monkey' which one can only assume is some sort of aggressive, courtship dance. At which point, m'learned friends intervene.

Michael Jackson, 'Beat It'

Howard be thy name.

This take on the Lord's Prayer is a fairly common one. 'Harold' is a variation. Howard's (or Harold's) all over the world can rejoice at their deification and blush at the daily invocation of their name. The mishearing comes mainly from children for whom, understandably, the word 'hallowed' is a little obscure.

The Lord's Prayer

Well, it changed right after the war. There was a **human cry** for some Black promotions in Asbury Park. As a result of the **human cry**, a group of young men got together and pressured the counsel.

'Hue and cry' is an extremely old expression, dating well back to the thirteenth century; where 'hue' meant the outcry in pursuit of a criminal of some sort – with a sense that it (the hue) was an inarticulate sound made by a horn or some other instrument. Dickens used it in *Oliver Twist*: 'But the old gentleman was not the only person who raised the hue-and-cry.' The two words were combined to make a phrase used by lawyers. 'Human cry' is an excellent variation on the theme that leads you to imagine just the rabble (or should that be 'rubble' – see below) pursuing and shouting, 'Exit pursued by human cry'.

www.visitmonmouth.com

🌴 Eggcorn　　🍍 Malapropism　　🦎 Mondegreen

I also have picked a secretary for Housing and **Human** Development. Mel Martinez from the state of Florida.

In this instance, I *think* Dubya meant 'Housing and Urban Development' but the remarkable thing about him is that sometimes he blunders onto something quite interesting. So, why not combine housing and human development? We spend so much time indoors – we could look to adapt ourselves and our living spaces to fit better? If this is not what he meant, Mel Martinez has a rather large job ahead of him. Actually, he may have already started on the Human Development – Bush warned famously in his 2006 State of the Union Address against 'human–animal hybrids'. The meaning of that phrase is still obscure, perhaps the Secretary for Housing and Human Development can explain?

 You picked a fine time to leave me Lucille, four **hundred** children and a crop in the field.

In that situation, no time is a 'fine' time to be packing your bags. Mind you, if Lucille has had four hundred children, I think she's entitled to a little time off. What I like about this image is Kenny Rogers, sitting in a field, surrounded by four hundred children and he's worrying about the crop! The original lyric is 'hungry'.

Kenny Rogers, 'Lucille'

 Liverpool will be without Kvarme tonight – he's **illegible**.

Jimmy Armfield here commentating on a Premiership match in the late 1990s and clearly having problems with his eyesight.

 What are you **incinerating**, Harold?

For many, *Steptoe and Son* was the definitive television sitcom of the 1960s. Albert and Harold Steptoe made up a good proportion of whatever the equivalent of water-cooler chat was in those days. The writers, Galton and Simpson, wrote this wonderful malapropism for insinuating which highlights both Albert's lack of education and his fiery personality.

Steptoe and Son

 For the second straight year, **inclimate** weather has caused the UIS men's basketball team to miss at least one game.

A new adjective which is growing in popularity. While the construction isn't attractive, the possible meaning – weather so bad it's not part of the normal climate – is useful; particularly in the current inclimate climate.

goprairiestars.athleticsite.com

Finally, we regret that the new cloakroom has not yet been completed due to the gross **incontinence** of the workmen we are using – the mess they leave is unbelievable! We apologise for this, and for this reason all members arriving wearing a coat will be asked to leave their coats behind the bar.

Enough said: if I were a patron I'd want to leave my coat behind the bar regardless of whether the cloakroom is finished or not. (See also DIRE REAR and INCONTINENT.)

 [The National Coal Board] are totally **incontinent**.

An accusation made at a time of high emotion during the Miners' Strike of 1984/5 on the *Today* programme by a leading National Union of Miners official. There are different ways of reading this terrific malapropism: did they have verbal diarrhoea, was the accusation that they were old and past it, or were they unable to control basic bodily functions? As so often with good malapropisms, the word that slips out says so much more about the situation than the intended word would have done.

 Stanley: We heard the sea is **infactuated** with sharks.
Oliver: Not infactuated. He means **infuriated**.

In the 1934 film *The Live Ghost*, Laurel and Hardy are persuaded to join a ship which is apparently haunted. Cue much nerve-tingling music and ghost jokes. Then we get a double malapropism to show what terrible sailors the duo will be. The sea may be 'infactuated' or 'infuriated' but both are better than it being 'infested' with sharks.

Laurel and Hardy *The Live Ghost*

 Eggcorn   Malapropism   Mondegreen

And he's missed … and some people gathered around my television screen here are jumping up and down in an **infanticide** way.

Football provokes extreme emotions – joy, heartache and boredom – and, sometimes, violence. I'm not aware, though, of any Herod-like attacks on opposing fans; Archie McPherson, in this example, needs to check his dictionary before making any further accusations.

Ah, but what you must remember is that the Pope is **inflammable**.

Religious leaders can be many things – inspirational, awe-inspiring, mesmerising. Rarely, though, do they self-combust. This is another Archie Bunkerism from the US sitcom *All in the Family*. If you're in a religious argument and you don't know how to get out of it, this is a model exit line.

All in the Family

insinuendo

A combination of 'innuendo' and 'insinuations', this is a great example of the art of the eggcorn. That said, the OED has refused to allow it, with the eminent lexicographer Robert Burchfield calling it 'a tasteless word'. It is first recorded in 1885 in *Longman's Magazine*, 'Could I not damn with faint praise and stab with sharp insinuendo?' in an article by one B. Matthews. Tasteless or not, a word which combines two such suggestive words is an excellent addition to the arsenal of words to be used by villains or other unpleasant characters.

Breakdown is for all **intensive purposes** a solid game.

While 'intents' used on its own to mean the object of an action or its aim is becoming rarer, it survives in the expression 'to all intents and

---

🌱 Eggcorn   🍍 Malapropism   🦗 Mondegreen

purposes' which itself dates back to at least the sixteenth century. However, the loss of the meaning of the word on its own pushes people to seek alternative and common words to replace it. 'Intensive' is a word that is still used very frequently and is an easy one to grasp. It also lays more stress on 'purposes' making the phrase more powerful. There is another variation which is also gaining ground which is 'for all intense purposes' which is really very (or intensely?) specific.

www.nlgaming.com

 Barbarous Monster! How have I deserved that my Passion should be resulted and treated with **Ironing**.

Thus a practised language mangler (Mrs Slipslop, the passionate housekeeper) in Fielding's *Joseph Andrews*. Mrs Slipslop is a marvellous creation. An expert malapropist in the finest tradition, she manages here to undermine any intellectual pretensions she has by using a word more fitting to her situation. So, 'irony' becomes 'ironing' in which case sarcasm could be scrubbing and hyperbole, hoovering.

Henry Fielding, *Joseph Andrews*

Bring me an **iron lung**.

Steve Winwood's 1986 hit 'Higher Love' is about the need to find true love in your life because 'Things look so bad everywhere/In this whole world, what is fair?' The solution, at least to one listener, is an artificial respirator. For many that may be the case but perhaps Winwood had loftier ideals in mind?

Steve Winwood, 'Higher Love'

Israeli men! Hallelujah! Israeli men.

The Weathergirls' 'It's Raining Men' will never be the same again. I can't get this one out of my mind now that I've heard it. The video to the original one-hit wonder showed the two large singers (their

🌱 Eggcorn　　🏺 Malapropism　　🦂 Mondegreen

former band name was 'Two Tons of Fun') announcing in the weather slot on the news that 'Tonight at about half past ten, for the first time in history' something extraordinary will happen. Unexpectedly the event is a deluge of Israeli men for some; plain 'men' for others. The mondegreen does all the right things: it scans, it works in the context, it sounds like the actual words and it changes the meaning of the song – in this instance in a delightfully absurd twist. Finally, it is apparently Homer Simpson's favourite song: what else can you ask for?

The Weather Girls, 'It's Raining Men'

 Eggcorn   Malapropism   Mondegreen

 Jack of all traits.

The original phrase 'jack of all trades' has been around since about the beginning of the seventeenth century. This new variation works on a different level: 'jack of all trades' exemplifies the manual nature of work in days gone by; 'jack of all traits' suggests a consummate 'yes-man' (otherwise known as an estate agent).

I was in **jail** just before we met.

This Abba song about someone who has suddenly turned into a obsessively jealous lover, from being a mild 'couldn't-care-less' kind of woman, is undermined if you mishear the first line as this. The opening of the song actually reads: 'I wasn't jealous before we met.' All of a sudden, the song is cast in a sinister light, with the narrator confessing to a life of stalking and preying on her victims. You wouldn't have thought it of Agnetha, would you?'

Abba, 'Lay All Your Love On Me'

JADEISMS

Jade Goody sprang to notoriety during the third series of *Big Brother* in 2002 and then reappeared in *Celebrity Big Brother* in 2007, which you may recall made one or two newspaper headlines. She has sprinkled some memorable phrases and malapropisms on the language which someone has christened 'Jadeisms'.

You'll **interiate**.

This is a very curious creation. Rather than 'deteriorating', she suggests that the person will consume him- or herself.

I'm not being **tintactical** here.

I like this word although I have absolutely no idea how she got to it. Presumably the intention was to say 'tactical' and yet the rogue prefix 'tin' elbowed its way to the front somehow. However it formed in her mind, 'tintactical' is a good word, whatever it means.

In the olden days they had **wirelophones** and they got music out of that.

A curious coinage – clearly based on 'wireless' but after that, who knows? 'Olden days' is of course relative – in this case I think she means the twentieth century which was, oh, years ago.

Where's **East Angular** though? I thought that was abroad.

Citizens of the Wash watch out, there's a redrawing of the map and there are two points to worry about: a) you're being renamed; and b) you're being lopped off the British Isles and deposited somewhere else. You have been warned.

Eggcorn   Malapropism   Mondegreen

To finish, here's one she probably got right but didn't know it.

 They were trying to use me as an **escape goat**.

This is from the 2002 series and is perhaps not the first time the phrase has been used. It is, though, the most widely quoted example. In fact the origins of the current accepted phrase 'scapegoat' point to 'escape goat' being perfectly admissible; 'scape' is a shortened form of 'escape' and so 'escape goat' makes clear the origins of the word. Good on you, Jade.

Kk

I feel like **Kevin** when I look in your eyes.

And what does that feel like? Pretty grim if the legend of Saint Kevin is anything to go by – he lived alone perched on a rock for seven years before establishing a monastery and, so the legend goes, being pretty vile to everyone and, particularly, women. (Apparently, up until the nineteenth century, the name Kevin was synonymous with someone who hated women.) Going back to the mondegreen, all this does not make for a promising relationship whereas the real lyric, entirely appropriate as boy-band fodder, was 'I feel in heaven when I look in your eyes'.

Backstreet Boys, 'Get Down'

Finally we filled each carriage with our creations and assorted candy canes and lollypops, and placed the whole **kit and caboose** on the dining table as our centre piece for our festive week.

Normally we say 'kit and caboodle' or the 'whole caboodle' but why? It's an expression that has almost no relevance to modern life and whose meaning is not at all apparent. That said, the 'kit and caboose' isn't any better except that a little delving reveals that 'caboose' means the cook-room on the deck of a ship. So at least there is the (tenuous) link with the kitchen sink.

Life is bigger/Bigger than you/And you are **knock-kneed**.

One of the most mondegreened songs of all time, REM's 'Losing My Religion' offers up some choice mishearings. This is one of my favourites: here's Michael Stipe putting someone in their place – you're just a small part of this vast thing called life – and, what's more, here comes the coup de grâce, you've got dodgy knees. Well, that told him. The actual line is 'And you are not me'.

REM, 'Losing My Religion'

You hardly talk to me anymore, when I **kung fu** the door at the end of the day.

Well, it has to be said that if you are in such a temper when you come home from work, conversation, let alone flowers, is a bit of an ask. Neil 'Bruce Lee' Diamond wrote this song in 1977 and he sang it at the Grammys in 1978 with Barbara Streisand. But instead of hearing 'come through' many heard 'kung fu'. Sadly neither appeared in kung fu gear to act out this great mishearing – Diamond then wrote a song which tried to put this image to rest: 'Forever in Blue Jeans'. However, in one of those neat coincidences that you stumble across, many heard 'Reverend Blue Jeans' instead which paints an altogether different picture of Diamond. From black belt to curate in two songs.

Neil Diamond, 'You Don't Bring Me Flowers'

🌴 Eggcorn 　🕯 Malapropism 　🐜 Mondegreen

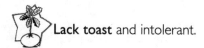

Lack toast and intolerant.

If you wake up in a bad mood, don't get breakfast soon enough and are generally a complete pain, you can be described as 'lack toast and intolerant'; if your body cannot break down lactose (the main sugar found in milk) you are lactose intolerant. I'm 'lack toast and intolerant' unfortunately.

In **lame** man's terms.

There is no doubt that compared to an expert, a lame man is at just as great a disadvantage as a layman is. The eggcorned image of a hobbling man trying to keep up with a 'fit' expert is more immediate than the rather more difficult original 'layman' (or someone not in religious orders).

You're looking for somewhere to belong, you're standing on my **lawn**.

It's an option. Ace of Base had several huge hits but, unlike their Swedish compatriots Abba, have not achieved a separate chapter in music history; this is the only mondegreen I have come across from their songs unlike Abba whose songs have inspired hundreds. The actual line is the rather bland 'You're standing all alone' which makes the misheard version positively thrilling by comparison.

Ace of Base, 'Beautiful Life'

 I have to say it delivers **leaps over bounds**.

Bounds and leaps can be synonyms but 'bounds' can also mean the boundary or edge of a territory (as in 'out of bounds') so presumably the writer here had the image of someone jumping the perimeter fence and plunging into unknown territory.

Street **lights**, they're the only **lights** I know.

Another favourite of mine: a graphic description of the dangers and thrills of 'living rough' becomes a meditation by a Highways Engineer on one aspect of his job. It takes the song off in a completely different direction and must be one of the few songs to put street furniture at its centre. Randy Crawford was in fact singing about 'street life'.

Randy Crawford, 'Street Life'

I'm not talking about the **linen**, and I don't want to change your life.

This 1976 hit for England Dan and John Ford Coley was straight out of the soft-rock academy (think Bread, Chicago and Gordon Light-foot if you want some fellow students) and was the kind of limp, grim easy listening that punk had as its target. 'Talking about the linen' could easily have fitted into the song given just how mundane it all is. The opening lines amount to 'nothing's happened, haven't seen you for a while' which promises about as much excitement as you get in the rest of the song. The real lyric is 'I'm not talkin' about movin' in'.

England Dan and John Ford Coley,
'I'd Really Love To See You Tonight'

 Eggcorn   Malapropism   Mondegreen

This is my brother's friends **lipsinging** 'We are the champions' by Queen.

The ugly phrase 'lip sync' was coined when live television performances started to become a rarity. How much more appealing that business would have been if we'd used the excellent word 'lipsing' to describe it. If you go on to YouTube or MySpace now you can't move for people proudly exhibiting their lipsinging prowess.

video.google.com

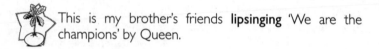 Well, that's all for now. I'll be watching on Monday to get the **load down** on the spy murder mystery...

Given the prevalence of downloading perhaps it is not surprising that this alternative to 'getting the low-down' has sprung up. In fact it's entirely appropriate for our digital age; either that or it could be yet another HR directive about health and safety in the office.

www.cnn.com

I get **locked out**, so I go out again.

Chumbawamba had a moment of fame in 1998 when one of the band's members poured a jug of water over Deputy Prime Minister John Prescott at the *NME* Music Awards. Self-styled anarchists, the band had already been formed for over fifteen years when this took place and lent them some notoriety. 'Tubthumping' was riding high at the time too and was taken up as something of an anthem for anarchists and protestors in general. What is great about this mondegreen is that the song in support of the oppressed ('I get knocked down but I get up again') is changed into a little domestic drama.

Chumbawamba, 'Tubthumping'

Eggcorn   Malapropism   Mondegreen

The judge in the town's got **love stains** on his pants.

'The Night the Lights Went Out in Georgia' is a curious song about a newly wed husband returning after a two-week absence. He stops at a bar and meets his best friend who tells him that his wife has been having an affair with someone else and that the best friend has also 'been with her himself'. Welcome back. The best friend is discovered dead by the husband who is then incorrectly convicted of killing him and hanged. It transpires that the song's narrator is the husband's sister and that she is responsible for the murder. This mishearing follows the line 'Don't trust your soul to no back woods southern lawyer', so it makes excellent sense in the context and adds a level of intrigue to this bizarre narrative. The actual line is equally damning: 'Cause the judge in the towns got bloodstains on his hand.' It all begs for CSI to turn up and work it all out – in about ten minutes.

Vicki Lawrence, 'The Night the Lights Went Out in Georgia'

All my **luggage** I will send to you.

In the 1960s, it appears, the basis for a demonstration of undying commitment was a complete set of suitcases. Pagan? Unsophisticated? Unusual, certainly. The mondegreen warrants selection if only for the picture of truck-load of Samsonites arriving at Linda's door with Paul singing 'All my luggage I have sent to you'.

The Beatles, 'All My Loving'

Eggcorn   Malapropism   Mondegreen

LORRAINE

A brief interlude on the person who probably most intrudes on songs. Lorraine crops up whenever the weather is bad which is probably due to the fact that an American accent can make 'the rain' and 'Lorraine' sound very similar.

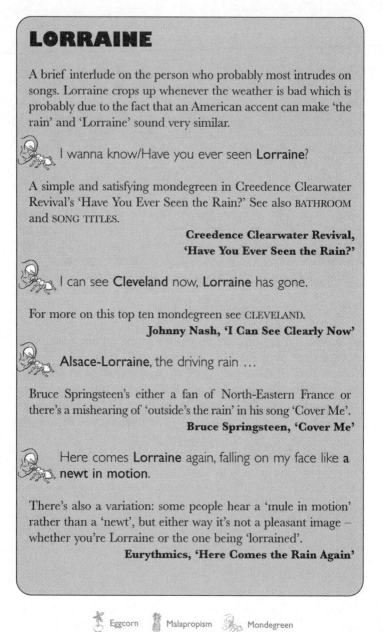 I wanna know/Have you ever seen **Lorraine**?

A simple and satisfying mondegreen in Creedence Clearwater Revival's 'Have You Ever Seen the Rain?' See also BATHROOM and SONG TITLES.

**Creedence Clearwater Revival,
'Have You Ever Seen the Rain?'**

I can see **Cleveland** now, **Lorraine** has gone.

For more on this top ten mondegreen see CLEVELAND.

Johnny Nash, 'I Can See Clearly Now'

Alsace-Lorraine, the driving rain …

Bruce Springsteen's either a fan of North-Eastern France or there's a mishearing of 'outside's the rain' in his song 'Cover Me'.

Bruce Springsteen, 'Cover Me'

Here comes **Lorraine** again, falling on my face like **a newt in motion**.

There's also a variation: some people hear a 'mule in motion' rather than a 'newt', but either way it's not a pleasant image – whether you're Lorraine or the one being 'lorrained'.

Eurythmics, 'Here Comes the Rain Again'

🐜 Eggcorn 🐜 Malapropism 🐜 Mondegreen

Mm

 With men and women, does you think that men should marry only one woman? Does you believe in **mahogany**?

This from an interview that Ali G had with John Gray (author of *Men Are From Mars, Women Are From Venus*). He goes on to ask why in some religions, 'like the Morons', it is acceptable to have more than one wife. Gray is admirably unfazed by the ease with which the malapropisms trip from Ali G's tongue. Ali G's relationship with English is challenging but the oblique angle he attacks it from makes for some great mis-speakings.

You Make Me Feel Like a **Man and A** Woman.

I love this take on Aretha Franklin's absolute classic from 1967 'You Make Me Feel Like a Natural Woman'. Turning the conviction of the actual title and lyrics on its head, the mishearing either expresses the singer's confusion over her sexuality or allows her the apparent delight of having the best of both worlds – being both male and female. It hardly matters: to rejoice in the androgynous state is a far cry from simply feeling 'like a natural woman'.

Aretha Franklin, 'You Make Me Feel Like a Natural Woman'

The Pitchfork is always on, and is **manner from heaven** for lovers of straw coloured hoppy ales. Hard to beat? Nay impossible.

This from a review of a pub which serves 'Pitchfork' beer. The original phrase is 'manna from Heaven' where 'manna' was miraculously provided as sustenance to the Israelites in the wilderness after their departure from Egypt. Manner from heaven is more likely to be a saintly disposition which could, I suppose, be applied to a beer.

www.beerintheevening.com

 I've been **eating marigolds.**

As chat-up lines go, it isn't really up there, is it? Imagine the orange petals stuck between the slightly gappy teeth of a lop-sided smile. Now compare with Hot Chocolate's original line 'I believe in miracles' – doesn't quite have the dramatic 'I had a religious moment as soon as I saw you' kind of ring to it, does it?

Hot Chocolate, 'You Sexy Thing'

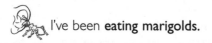 'But I will say, and I would if I was led a **Martha** to the Stakes for it,' Mrs Gamp remarked below stairs, in a whisper, 'that she don't look much like a merry one at this present moment of time.'

Martha is traditionally the image of domestic competence and energy. She embodied the Victorian picture of the perfect housewife. Sarah (Sairey) Gamp does not quite fit the bill: see PERSECUTION for her practices. Dickens comically highlights the insincerity of the character by pointing out her lack of self-knowledge and mis-speaking 'Martha' for 'martyr'.

Charles Dickens, *Martin Chuzzlewit*

Eggcorn   Malapropism   Mondegreen

I was only joking when I said I'd like to **mash a beetroot in your hair**.

I can't imagine Morrissey ever being angry. He is the picture of gloomy sufferance. So when, in 'Bigmouth Strikes Again', he admits he was only joking when he said 'I'd like to smash every tooth in your head', it's a relief. Better still is if you mishear the line as above.

The Smiths, 'Bigmouth Strikes Again'

Meatball, meatball, hit that perfect meatball

Bronski Beat's song 'Hit that Perfect Beat' is a mid-80s dance classic and gay anthem. It has nothing to do with cooking, Italian restaurants or abuse of Italian dishes. Some though hear the song as an exhortation to pummel meatballs repeatedly and destroy their perfection. One wonders why anyone would want to sing about a perfect meatball in the first place. The actual line is 'Beat boy beat boy hit that perfect beat boy'.

Bronski Beat, 'Hit that Perfect Beat'

Oh Lord, please don't let me be **Miss Sunday School**.

For all of us who suffered at the hands of a bossy Sunday school teacher, this is an understandable fear. The Animals though had a bigger message to convey: the plea of all miserable teenagers to their parents: 'please don't let me be misunderstood'.

The Animals, 'Don't Let Me Be Misunderstood'

He certainly didn't **mix** words as he described the ups and downs of the acting profession.

The phrase 'I didn't mince my words' means I didn't tone down my language to avoid offending someone and it derives the idea that when something is minced it is weakened or made light of. In the same way, 'mix' is being used to show that the words have not been adulterated and thereby weakened. This is an eggcorn that will become more and more common.

www.imdb.com

🌱 Eggcorn 🐜 Malapropism 🐜 Mondegreen

Just one of those things … even if you've gone over the list hundreds of times you're bound to miss some small **Monday** detail.

Details can often be dull and humdrum ('mundane' indeed), perhaps even annoying. No surprise then that writer associates them with the Monday – traditionally the worst day of the working week – a day perhaps when you are not at your most alert.

She keeps a **mower and shotgun**/in a pretty cabinet.

'Killer Queen' is one of those songs (like 'Bohemian Rhapsody' in fact) that begs to be misheard. Whether it is Freddie Mercury's voice or the rather obscure ideas he writes (the original is 'her Moet et Chandon'), it's also true that a lot of Queen's songs attract mondegreens. The first verse in which this one occurs tries to portray the Killer Queen as a model of ice-cold sophistication. What a shame then to put up the image of the mud-spattered gumbooted farmer traipsing around with a (motor?) mower and a shotgun. Not exactly what Freddie had in mind, I'm sure.

Queen, 'Killer Queen'

That's me with the **mower**/that's me with the **frostbite**.

As has been remarked elsewhere, Michael Stipe's diction leaves something to be desired; in 'Losing My Religion' some have clearly heard the song as if it is the singer who is losing his faith in that established area of worship: the garden. We all pray at that green altar – the rockery. The actual words, for what they're worth, are, 'That's me in the corner, that's me in the spotlight'.

REM, 'Losing My Religion'

Eggcorn   Malapropism   Mondegreen

Blown it for Ferrari!!! ... Blown it for Irvine!!! ... I don't know what happened, but there was a major **malmisorganisation** problem there!!!

Murray Walker, as he might have said, was so unique they only made one of him. Excitable to the point of eruption, he is one of the most famous sports commentators who has made many fevered additions to our lexicon – a classic Colemanball was 'and you can almost cut the tension with a cricket stump' – but here he exhibits a rare Germanic tendency of lumping word parts together to get over just what a cock-up he had witnessed. Had he invented Mrs Malaprop, maybe she would have become Mrs Malmisaprop or, even, a man: Major Malmisaprop. There was another occasion where his grammatical knowledge came to the fore: 'And Derek Warwick is driving an absolutely pluperfect race', and I don't suppose you can get much better than that.

Lahey was my mother's **mating** name ...

Ricky in *Trailer Park Boys*, a Canadian comedy series, is the equivalent of our own Del Boy in his verbal dexterity. Perhaps this is what his mother used in the Personal Ads?

Ricky, *Trailer Park Boys*

Every time you go away, you take a piece of **meat** with you.

Habitual thieving from the fridge is not the best basis for a relationship and invariably leads to arguments in student house-holds. That said, gradually taking a piece of your partner ('me') as in the original song is not ideal either.

Paul Young, 'Every Time You Go Away'

Eggcorn   Malapropism   Mondegreen

THE ORIGINAL MRS MALAPROP

While not the first to spot the fact that people often mis-speak, Richard Sheridan gave the art form a name by inventing Mrs Malaprop (in *The Rivals*) who uses 'her select words so ingeniously misapplied, without being mispronounced'. Some people now take issue with him because malapropisms (from the French *mal à propos* – not to the purpose) should not be linked to a mistake: more often than not malapropisms are creative and very much to the purpose. Sheridan's play *The Rivals* introduced the character of Mrs Malaprop to the audience as an 'old, weather-beaten she-dragon'. The pretentious would-be fixer of Lydia Absolute's romantic future announces her intention to 'illiterate' the wooer of her niece before laying waste to the English language. Some famous malapropisms are shown below:

***Illiterate him**, I say, quite from your memory.*

*She's as headstrong as an **allegory** on the banks of the Nile.*

*No caparisons, Miss, if you please – **Caparisons** don't become a young woman.*

*If I **reprehend** any thing in this world, it is the use of my **oracular** tongue, and a nice **derangement** of **epitaphs**!*

The culmination of this language massacre is a superb speech in which she lectures her brother about what a girl's education should consist of.

Mrs Malaprop. *Observe me, Sir Anthony. I would by no means wish a daughter of mine to be a **progeny** of learning; I don't think so much learning becomes a young woman … But, Sir Anthony, I would send her, at nine years old, to a boarding-school, in order to learn a little ingenuity and artifice. Then, sir, she should have a **supercilious** knowledge in accounts; – and as she grew up, I would have her instructed in geometry, that she might know something of the **contagious** countries; – but above all, Sir Anthony, she should be mistress of **orthodoxy**, that she might* *not mis-spell, and mis-pronounce words so shamefully as girls usually do; and likewise that she might* **reprehend** *the true meaning of what she is saying. This, Sir Anthony, is what I would have a woman know; – and I don't think there is a* **superstitious** *article in it.*

Finally, to show that even this well-known character and her idiosyncratic behaviour are not immune to a bit of malapropism, here's a quote from the *New Scientist* where a contributor confessed:

I've committed a Miss Marple-ism.

Which opens a whole new area of linguistic invention.

You can kick your heels up and enjoy yourself, very important, you've got to get out and relieve the **monopoly**.

Which sounds like a call to arms to fight against a state-owned business. Monopolies can be tedious no doubt about it but on the whole it's preferable to be relieved of the monotony. Anyone who has played interminable games of Monopoly as parents will also want a chance to 'relieve the monopoly'.

agricultured.gn.apc.org

Bless the babe, and save the mother, is my **mortar**, sir; but I makes so free as add to that, Don't try no impogician with the Nuss, for she will not abear it!

Sarah Gamp in *Martin Chuzzlewit* constructs a bomb out of a maxim and all who hear it shudder – including the babe, the mother and the person thinking to engage her. She meant to say, of course, 'motto'.

Charles Dickens, *Martin Chuzzlewit*

Eggcorn   Malapropism   Mondegreen

MOST MISHEARD SONG LYRICS

There is one line in rock/pop history which stands out as the most misheard of all time. Sad case that I am, I spent an entire evening with some friends trying to decipher the lyrics to REM's 'The Sidewinder Sleeps Tonight'. We got perhaps 90 per cent of it but got utterly stuck on one line. The line is 'Call me when you wake her up'. I was convinced that the sidewinder was actually the coiled metal wire that attaches the telephone to the metal money box in a public telephone. Stipe sings 'There's scracthes around the coin slot' and 'But this machine only swallows money' – both lines seemed to endorse my increasingly heated conviction that the whole song was about telephoning someone to wake them up. The disputed line was therefore 'Coin in to wake her up'. Elaborate perhaps but positively pedestrian compared to some of the reworked song lyrics listed below.

Call me Jim Bakker.

Call your time, Abraham.

Calling each other a wanker.

Come 'n' eat Jamaican bread.

Come again, try to wake her up.

Come and eat your bacon up.

Commie Tammy Fay Bakker

Comin' in 'Ciao, Bakker'

Goin' to Jamaica.

Only in Jamaica, mon.

Fryin' up some back-bacon

Tokin' on some Jamaican

Tony Chawayga ga ga.

Tony shall wait for her.

Eggcorn   Malapropism   Mondegreen

> *Don't even try to wake her up*
> *Only in Jamaica, hah*
> *Call me Cheryl Baker*
> *Call me when you get to Chatuaqua.*
> *Calling Cheryl Baker up*
> *Promise I'd wait for her*
> *Calling Jamaica*
> *Calling Chuck the baker*

I **mow the lawn** for your affection./Tell me now that that ain't so.

Def Leppard's agonised wail about the perils of falling in love, 'Breathe a Sigh', gets a horticultural makeover in this mishearing with the high-flown exclamations of eternal love replaced by the high-pitched whine of the hover-mower. The real words are 'I more than long for your affection./I tell you now that that ain't so'.

Def Leppard, 'Breathe a Sigh'

Wise guys realise there's danger in her **muscular thighs**.

George Michael wrote 'Young Guns' as a warning to man about the hazard of settling down when you're too young; not, as some people hear, a warning about a girlfriend who spends too much time in the gym. The danger was from 'emotional ties' in the song.

Wham!, 'Young Guns'

If we're going to maintain America's status as the number one maritime power ... it means having modern **musicians** and well-trained soldiers.

Michael Dukakis famously lost the Presidential race in 1988 to George Bush Snr after Bush had mocked his liberal views on capital

 Eggcorn Malapropism Mondegreen

punishment. His defeat, given the above gaffe, is not that surprising if he thinks that an orchestra is an integral part of modern naval warfare. To be fair, Dukakis did correct himself immediately by saying 'munitions'.

To your question about the competency of our legions, all members must pass **mustard** using a number of standard hand guns and light anti-tank weapons.

'Muster' has dropped out of everyday use. It means, usually in a military context, a coming together for inspection which is seldom heard or seen these days. When an expression containing that word is used more frequently than the word itself, the word becomes unfamiliar and people often turn to a similar sounding word as a substitute. The word that is drafted in is used in an expression not unlike the original phrase. 'Cut the mustard' has been broken up to complete the phrase in this instance.

krow.livejournal.com

Maybe this is a **mute point** because they all lock down the client machines instead of working through the ISP or the network level.

This is classic eggcorn territory. 'A moot point' is a point of law which is open to discussion and debate. The phrase (and the word moot used as a noun) go back to at least the sixteenth century; the legal use of 'moot' on its own died off and the phrase 'moot point' became idiomatic but its origins became more and more obscure as 'moot' fell out of use. All it needs is a current, similar-sounding word to be available for a new phrase to be born. So, a 'mute point' comes into being.

www.techdirt.com

Eggcorn   Malapropism   Mondegreen

Nn

 Betty was straight as a **narrow**, totally transparent, nothing behind a veil.

In a moving obituary to an 85-year-old woman, we get a new expression – and a good one. While 'straight as an arrow' may have been relevant to Maid Marion, we now need something more modern. 'Straight as a narrow' fills that gap by substituting bowls (and curling) for archery. When you play something 'narrow' in bowls, the line along which the bowl is bowled is too close to the target for the natural bias to come into effect – hence the bowl goes nearly straight; or straight as a narrow …

Stop! in the **neighborhood** before you break my heart.

The Supremes' 1965 hit is one of the great Motown records, which has been endlessly covered. It also has one of those moments of choreography that is also forever being copied: hand on the hip, other hand outstretched in a 'stop' position. The song itself is about a two-timing boyfriend and when you listen to it with 'in the neighborhood' in your head, it makes a lot of sense: 'Each time you leave my door/I watch you walk down the street/knowing your other love you'll meet'.

The Supremes, 'Stop! In the Name of Love'

NATIONAL ANTHEMS

Whether it is because they are deemed important or whether it is because they are heard 'live' a lot more than other songs, national anthems have not prompted a huge number of mishearings. Those that I have encountered are listed below:

O Canada, we stand on **cars and freeze**...
Instead of the actual line:
O Canada, we stand on guard for thee ...

'O Canada'

The opening of 'Advance Australia Fair' seems to be problematic for a lot of people:

Australians all **love ostriches,/four minus one is three**
Australians all **are sausages** ...

have all been offered as alternatives to the actual lines
Australians all let us rejoice/For we are young and free

And the fourth line has this perfectly logical alternative version:

Our **land is dirt** *by sea*

to the real lyric:

Our home is girt by sea.

'Advance Australia Fair'

'The Star-Spangled Banner' has provoked two excellent mishearings:

José *can you see by the dawn's early light*
What so proudly we hailed as the twilight's **blasphemy**?
instead of:

Oh, say can you see by the dawn's early light
What so proudly we hailed at the twilight's last gleaming?

How the twilight blasphemed is not made clear.

🌴 Eggcorn 🌱 Malapropism 🐜 Mondegreen

It was extremely **nerve-wrecking** on the first day of rehearsals but everyone has been so accepting and welcoming.

Singer Connie Fisher updates a time-honoured expression to make it comprehensible to the modern world. While 'wrack' (and 'rack') meaning to ruin completely or to overthrow, this sense is not really heard nowadays; however, it is heard when we speak of 'wrecking' something. So 'he wrecked the car' or, indeed, a nervous wreck. A short step later we have 'nerve-wrecking'.

 She doesn't like me, and I don't like her, so it's **neutral**.

This, like many malapropisms, has an admirable logic. Of course mutual antipathy is 'neutral' – one hatred cancels out the other.

 Currently exploring the **never** regions of tech house and being influenced by DJs and artists such as Eddie Richards, Mr C, Nathan Coles, Terry Francis, Daniel Poli, Paul Stubbs and Dave Mothersole to name but a few.

Abandon all hope ye who enter here. That assumes that you get there in the first place. In place of the traditional 'nether regions' some mishear this to be 'never regions' which translates as 'Abandon all hope of ever getting here'. 'Nether regions' can allude to Hell or the nearest equivalent thereof, or, it seems only since the 1950s, what the OED primly describes as 'the lower part of the body'.

www.thedonton.co.uk

 Eggcorn   Malapropism   Mondegreen

'We take the dangers of alcohol seriously,' said Spangler. 'It's better to **nip it in the butt** sooner than later.'

The expression 'nip in the bud' was first recorded in the early seventeenth century (previously the expression was 'nip in the bloom'); the horticultural roots are clear in both cases. Nipping something in the 'butt' however is an entirely different proposition: a gratuitous act of crab-on-human violence?

Daily Nebraskan

The *New York Post* even had their **nipples** in a twist about the 'new look' of the band.

That would certainly be an extremely painful way of expressing your displeasure. While the original phrase 'getting your knickers in a twist' is starting to feel dated (some people have traced it only as far back as *The Basil Brush Show* in the late 1960s), this variation is an altogether more extreme way of venting your frustration.

Del: Most of those girls down there are the daughters of the **nobless**.

Rodney: What, Del?

Del: The nobless! The nobless! It's French for nobility.

A fine example of Del Boy's multilingualism, 'the nobless' are a rare class in France nowadays but history has recorded that they lost their heads under Madame Guillotine rather than another (equally vital) part of their anatomy.

Only Fools and Horses, 'The Russians are Coming'

 Eggcorn   Malapropism   Mondegreen

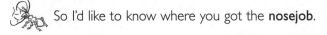 So I'd like to know where you got the **nosejob**.

Some claim that 'Don't Rock the Boat' was the first disco single to get to Number one in the US; it seems unlikely that in 1974 a song about plastic surgery would be so popular but that is how some people hear it. It's more interesting than the original line 'So I'd like to know where you got the notion' anyway.

Hues Corporation, 'Rock the Boat'

NURSERY RHYMES

A very brief selection of gaffes in the nursery:
Baa baa black sheep/ **Happy at the mall**
Updated for the shopping age, Baa Baa Black Sheep visits TK Maxx.

'Baa Baa Black Sheep'

Little Miss Muffet sat on a tuffet/Eating her **curtains away**.
'Little Miss Muffet'

London britches falling down, my **bare** lady.

A distinctly American take on an English favourite which paints a rather different picture, one not suitable for the nursery.
'London Bridge is Falling Down'

And one for the little boy that lives down the **drain**
And one for the little boy that lives down the lane.

 The **obfuscation of justice** by the government of India does not end there

Normally, those involved in holding up or preventing the legal process are simply obstructing it: they make things difficult, remain mute or refuse to co-operate. It is an entirely different matter to obfuscate it – although some people think that the legal profession are themselves rather adept at it. Dickens being one – the opening paragraphs of *Bleak House* describe the general fog over England and the particular one of the Court of Chancery which represents the system of justice of the time:

'And hard by Temple Bar, in Lincoln's Inn Hall, at the very heart of the fog, sits the Lord High Chancellor in his High Court of Chancery.'

There goes my hero, he's **old and hairy**.

Like Five for Fighting's 'Superman' (see FORNICATES) this is not the usual image of the hero. In this song 'My Hero' by The Foo Fighters, they too make no great claims for the object of their worship. Even in the original lyrics, the hero is only 'ordinary' but to some people that simply isn't modest enough; he's decrepit and hirsute too.

The Foo Fighters, 'My Hero'

Old timer's disease.

A slight cheat this one as, in general, the phrase is not mistakenly used but it is a neat mishearing of 'Alzheimer's Disease'. I included it because it is irresistible: when you have a name for a disease that mainly affects the elderly and the name can be adapted to such an apt alternative, you've struck linguistic gold.

 I was given an **old tomato**, leave or get thrown out ...

This alternative to 'ultimatum' is taken from the US TV sitcom *Will and Grace* and said with an American twang works very well. Why not threaten someone with an old tomato if your patience has been pushed to the limits?

 In the past, an **old wise tale** stated that amethyst prevented individuals from becoming overly intoxicated.

The expression 'old wives' tale' goes back to the sixteenth century and was used as a scornful rejection of any theory which seemed homespun and nonsensical. Over the last few decades numerous books have appeared which have collected and analysed these folkloric remedies and stories. Perhaps it is because these books do take the theories more seriously that 'old wise tale' is becoming more widely used. Alternatively, it is simply a mishearing which makes much sense if you have never heard of 'old wives' tales'.

Olive the other reindeer used to laugh and call him names.

There comes a time in every child's life when the truth about Christmas comes crashing into their consciousness. That there was a reindeer pulling the sled that answered to the rather pedestrian name of Olive (mishearing of 'all of') is perhaps not one of those moments, entertaining though it is. (See also CHRISTMAS box on p. 41.)

'Rudolf the Red-nosed Reindeer'

🌱 Eggcorn   🍍 Malapropism   🐜 Mondegreen

I want you **on top of me**.

The Buzzcocks' song 'Autonomy' features on their first album 'Another Kind of Music in a Different Kitchen', released in 1978. It's a pretty simple song, with few lyrics. However, a friend misheard the song chorus as a plea for more intimate relations rather than a demand for personal freedom. The actual line is simply 'I want you, autonomy'.

The Buzzcocks, 'Autonomy'

 Flying saucers are just an **optical conclusion**.

This has been attributed to the former holder of the title 'American Malaprop King' (until George W. took it and made it his own), Yogi Berra. However, I can find no evidence that he did say it and it may be one of those quotes where people feel he simply should have said it. It's a good malapropism, whatever. Berra did come out with the line 'You can see a lot just by observing', which might be said to be an 'optical conclusion'.

I need help on doing **outer body experiences**. By the way, does anyone know if remote viewing is connected to astral projections? I need steps on how to outer body experience.

The great thing about eggcorns is that they provide you with a new expression or word that you didn't even know you needed. For years, we have listened to people going on about their 'out of body experiences' or 'astral projections' or any one of the fifty or so words and expressions that have been coined (including my favourite 'psychonavigation'). Now it's time to bring it back to Earth a little and have simply an 'outer body experience' which can, presumably, be a massage or any other skin-related indulgence. I also like in the quote above that it is now a verb.

communities.anomalies.net

 Eggcorn   Malapropism   Mondegreen

You've **overgrown** your welcome.

By which point things are really bad presumably? The image of getting too big for the size of your welcome (when you outgrow it) is somewhat understated compared to this new phrase which describes how you have completely taken over the welcome like so much bindweed.

 Macario's wife is not the only one suspicious of his new-found capabilities, and she questions him as to whether he's made a **pack** with the Devil.

A simple eggcorn that adds to the stock of Devil expressions – this time gathering equipment for a hiking trip. The usual expression is 'pact with the Devil'.

www.classicfilmguide.com

 If they do not have the balance down **packed** you will see one system dominating another and that will not be good for this game.

The original phrase is 'to have something down pat' which means that you can do something faultlessly from memory by dint of endless practice. Instead, here and in other places, we see people using a variation which I assume comes from the idea that if you're packed then you are ready to go and everything is finalised or finished.

 It was two, tree miles down the road, I can't be too **pacific** but somewhere in that **virginity**.

This from a witness in a trial in the US. There's a deep satisfaction when two such fine examples of the malaproptic art burst into one sentence. Here, there's a statement that one can never be peace-loving enough followed by a new use of what the OED describes as 'The condition of being or remaining in a state of chastity'. Perhaps more appropriate would be if we all started to speak of 'preserving our vicinity'?

He won't last. He's just a flash in the **pants**.

The image conjured up by a well-known saying can lose its relevance to modern life. When we are so used to cooking in the oven and with microwaves, the regularity with which we encounter the flash of fat igniting in a frying pan is reduced. That being said, who really wants to have this new image floating around in their heads instead?

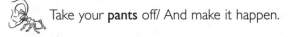

Take your **pants** off/ And make it happen.

The signature tune of the film *Flashdance … What a Feeling*, Irene Carr's 1983 hit went platinum, topped the Billboard Hot 100 chart and won an Academy Award for Best Original Song. It's a song about realising your dreams and, for all you grammar nerds out there, it is one of a very few song titles with an ellipsis in the title. Perhaps more appropriately for this mondegreen there was apparently a soft-porn version of the film made called *Fleshdance* – where this mishearing clearly belongs. The original words are 'take your passion and make it happen'.

Irene Carr, 'Flashdance … What a Feeling'

You're a **parasite** for sore eyes.

In the best tradition of malapropisms, this one by film actor and director Gregory Ratoff does more than simply substitute one word ('sight') for another: it enhances the original expression. Ratoff was Russian by birth and he used his accent to his advantage by playing roles that demanded broken English with a thick Eastern European growl. Given that, the parasite seems all the more threatening.

 Eggcorn   Malapropism   Mondegreen

Dorothy Macmillan: What are you looking forward to now?

Madame de Gaulle: **A penis**.

General de Gaulle: My dear, I think the English don't pronounce the word quite like that. It's not 'a penis', but 'appiness.

A slight cheat this one, but irresistible. While the majority of this book deals with native English speakers, Madame de Gaulle's gaffe merits inclusion on the grounds that it is such a blunder in such 'exalted' company. Imagine the shock waves in 1960s political circles as de Gaulle's wife mentioned the 'p-word'.

'There she identically goes! Poor sweet young creetur, there she goes, like a lamb to the sacrifige! If there's any illness when that wessel gets to sea,' said Mrs Gamp, prophetically, 'it's murder, and I'm the witness for the **persecution**.'

Sarah (Sairey) Gamp is a prize exponent of malapropism. Her consumption of 'half pint of porter ... that is bought reg'lar and draw'd mild' could well be a contributing factor to her verbal slips. In this instance, though there is more than a grain of truth in the gaffe: more often than not the law, seen through Dickens' eyes, presents a case for 'persecution' rather than 'prosecution'. See OBFUSCATION for more on his thoughts about the legal profession.

Charles Dickens, *Martin Chuzzlewit*

A **pigment** of the imagination.

This eggcorn is used by artists and photographers and has been around for some time. What's nice about it is that it adds an extra dimension to a well-worn phrase – as eggcorns often do.

Eggcorn   Malapropism   Mondegreen

I don't want to win? If that were the case, why the heck am I on the bus sixteen hours a day, shaking thousands of hands, giving hundreds of speeches, getting **pillared** in the press and cartoons and still staying on message to win?

See also the BUSHISMS box on p. 31. Another example of George W.'s unique take on the English language; only as consummate a malapropist as he would be able to take an expression still in widespread use and mangle it to come up with something as impressive as this. While other people are 'pilloried' by the press, George gets made into a supporting column.

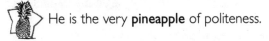 He is the very **pineapple** of politeness.

Mrs Malaprop has made many contributions to gaffery but this is the 'pineapple'. A stumble over 'pinnacle', 'the very pineapple of politeness' takes its place as one of the most enduring malapropisms. Does it mean that peaches are uncivil and apples downright rude? (See also MRS MALAPROP box on p. 100.)

 The only boy who could ever reach me was the son of a **pizza** man.

Dusty Springfield's memory of a son of the clergy (the original line is 'son of a preacher man') is a beautiful elegiac love song; what a pity some hear it as the prosaic son of the local after-the-pub delivery man. Extra cheese anyone?

Dusty Springfield, 'Son of a Preacher Man'

 We shall reach greater and greater **platitudes** of achievement.

Former Chicago Mayor Richard Daley has a few entries in this book. I like this one in particular because 'platitudes' (rather than 'plateaux') are exactly what he is uttering – although that is not what he wants the audience to think of course. See also ASPARAGUS and PRESERVE.

 Eggcorn   Malapropism   Mondegreen

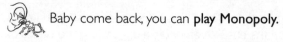

Baby come back, you can **play Monopoly.**

Player were formed in 1976 from members whose former bands included Palladin, Skyband, Count Zeppelin and his Fabled Airship (really) and Ice Follies. 'Baby Come Back' was a hit in 1978 after the two founder members had both split up with their girlfriends (maybe the girlfriends had heard the rehearsals?). Some people hear 'play Monopoly' instead of 'blame it all on me' but I'm not sure that anyone wants to listen again to check out how easy it is to confuse the two. Player's other crime was coining the phrase 'Rock 'n' Soul' to describe their music.

Player, 'Baby Come Back'

If you wanna be my **plumber**

Every now and again, someone comes up with a mishearing which is absolutely perfect; this is just such a one. Take the anthem of a decade (the 90s in this case) and subvert the exciting, sexy, fashion-setting message with something so domestic, so utilitarian and so utterly undesirable and you have a sure-fire top-notch alternative song. After all if you mistake 'lover' for 'plumber' then you are well on your way to undermining the whole basis of the song – and from there only monkey wrenches, leaking dishwashers, blocked toilets and downpipes can follow. The actual words are 'If you wanna be my lover'.

Spice Girls, 'Wannabe'

Portaloo, couldn't escape if I wanted to.

There is something about Abba that attracts the scatological mind. In this instance, we have a modern take on the famous battle of the song 'Waterloo' which does conjure a funny image of Napoleon hammering on the door of the battlefield toilet. (See also DIARRHOEA.)

Abba, 'Waterloo'

Eggcorn Malapropism Mondegreen

… the screenplay is about a female war journalist who returns to her Glasgow home from the Middle East with **post-dramatic** stress disorder after she puts her cameraman in serious danger.

Ever had that feeling after a particularly bad local production of *Twelfth Night* that you're in need of some serious psychological help? Never been able to describe the feeling properly? Well, help is at hand. With a little tweak of 'post-traumatic stress disorder', a proper term to describe the consequences of Am-Dram is created.

 Found an island in your arms,/**poultry** in your eyes.

Jim Morrison's lyrics were often chemically influenced so why not hear something as embellished as this compared with the more mundane 'country in your eyes'?

The Doors, 'Break on Through'

 Meanwhile, Richard Parker Bowles, brother of Camilla's ex-husband, Andrew, said that from the beginning Camilla approved of Charles marrying Diana while she remained his **power mower.**

This is quoted in Anne Fadiman's wonderful book *Ex Libris* from the *Richmond Times-Dispatch.* I do associate Prince Charles with all things green and organic and I'm sure he does have a very high-tech power mower but I'm doubtful that it could have been used in a court as grounds for divorce. Adultery has never been so well served as by this image of horticultural technology – and as a consequence I can't help but think of it whenever I hear the abused word 'paramour'.

Anne Fadiman, *Ex Libris*

🌴 Eggcorn   🐜 Malapropism   🐜 Mondegreen

pre-madonna.

A slight change of emphasis transforms the established 'prima donna' from the first lady of an operatic or ballet company into a word to describe the category of demanding, self-important temperamental performer who existed before the 1980s and a certain other 'material girl' (see also CHEERIO). A number of divas can be included, such as Maria Callas and Edith Piaf, but what is the term for those coming along now? Post-madonnas?

> The policeman is not there to create disorder, the policeman is there to **preserve** disorder.

Richard Daley's gift, when he was not throwing ASPARAGUS at his opponents, was to utterly bewilder his political adversaries. While some believe that the role of law enforcement is to keep the streets under control, Daley, in the best traditions of malapropism, suggests the opposite.

> Calvin: 'I'm so smart it's almost scary. I guess I'm a child **progeny**.'
>
> Hobbes: 'Most children are.'

Only a child prodigy would know the word in the first place I suppose.

Eggcorn   Malapropism   Mondegreen

PRESCOTTISMS

Linda Smith, the much-missed British comedian, once remarked of John Prescott that: 'I don't think language is his first language.' He could certainly challenge Chomsky's theory of deep grammar being innate in all of us. Prescott is famous for mangling his words to bewildering effect and his speeches are a mixture of every kind of linguistic gaffe – spoonerism, malapropism, mangled syntax, bizarre grammar - you name it, he is a master. As a final, if somewhat far-fetched, testament to his gaffe credentials, Prescott shares his name with George W.'s (rather more) illustrious grandfather Prescott Sheldon Bush.

 the **sceptre** of unemployment stalking the North East

I like the image of a royal insignia creeping around England, 'bestowing' unemployment on people – like a privilege.

 single-**finger** majorities

Prescott is renowned for his blunt, confrontational style – ask anyone who has tried to waylay him electioneering. Famously he also performed the two-finger salute to a group of journalists as he arrived for a Cabinet meeting in 2003. It is entirely in keeping that he describe any kind of numerical advantage in such an aggressive way.

 What we want is **an affair** and affordable pensions scheme.

This unfortunate slip-of-the-tongue happened at the time of the revelation of his liaison with Tracey Temple, his assistant private secretary.

Eggcorn   Malapropism   Mondegreen

And an example that George W. would surely have been proud of:

> For the first time hypothecating any real increase in fuel duty to roads and public transport and I invite them to say if this hypothecation they are compared to adopt it.

Having struggled manfully with 'hypothecation' and 'hypothecating' in one sentence, Prescott blows it all with a clause which simply falls apart. Apparently in 2002, officials were instructed to write answers for Prescott which were 'easily spoken aloud'. One wonders if they were listening.

This is not a game for the **puritans.**

So said Martin Tyler of Sky Sports – a commentator not prone to that many gaffes so they should be recorded when they come. In one sense, he is absolutely right: the modern sense of 'puritan' does include echoes of a disapproval of recreation, a strict view on sexual morality and the rejection of any flamboyant clothing; I can't think of any footballers of the last thirty years who conform to any of these ideas. However, I'm not sure that Tyler, in the heat of commentary, meant anything quite so elaborate. The word he may have been stretching for is 'purist'.

 **Pus** (pus, pus) and **phlegm** (phlegm, phlegm).

Pink Floyd's *Dark Side of the Moon* has been called many pretentious things – 'as much an aural collage as an art-rock treatise', for example. So it is entirely acceptable in my view to offer up this disgusting and very unpretentious mishearing to the self-indulgent

Eggcorn   Malapropism   Mondegreen

prog-rockers. The moody, ominous song 'Us and Them' about social difference is summed up in its title; how delicious then to find people who mishear this as a rather more basic social commentary which fits perfectly well with the line that follows, 'After all we're only ordinary men' – made of 'pus and phlegm' presumably.

Pink Floyd, 'Us and Them'

 My face is sore and I don't like having big **pus jewels** on my face.

I think we're all in agreement there. 'Pustules' are as disgusting in the flesh (apologies for this) as the word is on the ear. A black crust forming on a flea bite or spot was in a small number of cases the indication of the onset of the Black Death or bubonic plague which wiped out a good proportion of Europe in a number of outbreaks from the fourteenth to the eighteenth centuries. Estimates are as high as 75 million deaths. You really didn't want to wake up with a black spot on your face in those days. If, however, you were to wake up with pus jewels on your face perhaps that might have been some compensation. Worth trying the word out with depressed teenagers as well: how much less damaging to call the spotty face a treasure chest of pus jewels? OK, probably won't work.

 I don't deny it, I was most **putrified** with astonishment when you give me that smack.

If you're petrified, you've been turned to stone; if you're putrified, you're well on the way to decomposing completely and are also a bit whiffy. I think this is a very useful eggcorn for a different experience of fear – if you quiver and melt rather than become paralysed for example.

Mark Twain, *The Adventures of Huckleberry Finn*

 Eggcorn   Malapropism   Mondegreen

Love is a big, fat **quivering slug**.

This mishearing of Sting's original line 'Love is a big, fat river in flood' is one of the odder ones in music history. 'Love' has been compared to many things in songs, ranging from a heat wave, oxygen and a butterfly to Las Vegas and tears from the stars. Usually the connotation is positive and grand. In this instance, the listener clearly thinks the magic has gone for Sting. Either that or he has developed some strange fetishes over the years.

Sting, 'Love is Stronger than Justice'

Rr

Happy **as a rafter** in the market place.

Why choose the active life when you can be supported aloft for all your days? The prospect of idling away the years perched above the market may not be so dull after all – particularly in the acid-fuelled late 60s. This mishearing of the words 'happy ever after' in 'Ob la di' works well in the context of the song, and, in one of those nice little coincidences, the Marmalade version of the song which went to Number One in 1969, was succeeded at the top spot by 'Lily the Pink' by The Scaffold. Clearly there was a building theme developing in the charts at that time. 'Ob la di' was one of the oddest song titles The Beatles ever came up with; apparently it means 'life goes on' in.

Yaruba Beatles, 'Ob la di'

It allows him to give free **range** to his impulses as he works through the material.

The origins of the expression 'give free rein to' are in horse riding but the phrase quickly gained a figurative sense of allowing someone complete control. This eggcorn takes the expression in a slightly different direction by implying that someone can express themselves to the limits of their ability in addition to being in control.

www.albany.edu

Can somebody give me a sample of a hotel organisational chart from top management to **ranking file**?

A mishearing of the original expression 'rank and file' which arose from the body of non-commissioned soldiers when they were arrayed in square formation (in ranks and files in other words). The ranking file conjures up other images: the most respected iron file in the toolbox? I like the echo of an association with reggae: uptown top-ranking file.

answers.yahoo.com

 Tourists who come to visit us have the opportunity to enjoy the traditional culture of the region (mixture of Romanian, Greek, Macedonian and Turkish influences) as well as **reek the benefits** of the modern tourist facilities.

We can harvest or 'reap' the benefits or now we can 'reek' them. But while 'reap' lends the idea of something earned and planned for, reek gives us an entirely different picture. I think in this instance I might forgo the pleasures of the modern tourist facilities on olfactory grounds …

www.infoliteral.ro

 Maldini has really **regurgitated** his career at left-back

Damien Richardson, Irish pundit and former manager of many Irish football teams, is an unusually florid speaker – loading his comments with images from astrology and literature in a manner that makes Rococo architecture look demure. Here he goes for the short and pithy but mistakes 'regurgitated' for 'resurrected' and makes the listener feel equally nauseous: Maldini's former glory lies splattered over his boots, diced carrot and all.

 [Of a UK runner] She's really tough, she's **remorseful**.

It takes a lot to admit your mistakes: you need determination, mental strength and remorse. However, generally speaking, remorse is not

Eggcorn   Malapropism   Mondegreen

required to run: you don't need to feel a hint of guilt or even slightly apologetic to have a trot round the park. Dave Moorcroft, scrambling 'resourceful' here, ran UK Athletics until August 2006, presiding over the team's abject failure in that year's European Championships. Now there is perhaps a connection between running and remorse.

The actor says, "I am also doing a heart-**rendering** set on my life and the mistakes I have made."

David Hasselhoff here describing the musical of his life in which he is appearing. He replaces the usual 'heart-rending' meaning 'tearing' with a word that could produce any number of different images. At its worst, the picture is of the heart being boiled to produce oil which would be less heart-rending and more stomach churning – or should that be stomach curdling?

From the outset, I believe all of us have been deeply upset and **revulsed** by the statements that were made on air about the young women who represented Rutgers University in the NCAA Women's Basketball Championship with such class, energy and talent.

This from a statement by CBS President and CEO Les Moonves about a notorious US talk show host (Don Imus) who was sacked early in 2007 for making extremely offensive remarks about a woman's basketball team. 'Revulsed' hasn't yet made it into the OED in this sense (there is an entry but it is 'obsolete' and is defined as 'to drag or pull something back') but it is surely only a matter of time. A combination of 'repulsed' and 'revulsion', it's a good example of taking the familiar and twisting it slightly to great effect.

I see a **Renoir** and I want it painted black.

The Rolling Stones have been accused of many things in their long and glorious career but abject philistinism is not, to my knowledge, an accusation that has been levelled at them before. However, if you

Eggcorn   Malapropism   Mondegreen

listen to 'Paint it Black' you can see where the mishearing comes from. The original line is 'red door' which is more Howard Hodgkin than Renoir I'd have thought.

The Rolling Stones, 'Paint it Black'

My friend, what is it you find so darned mysterious about me that it has you in such constant **revelries**?

You can see this malapropism becoming more and more common. A 'reverie' is a daydream, a gentle daytime meditation or fancy, so it's not a huge step to describe a more intense and humorous musing as a 'revelry'.

Zadie Smith, *White Teeth*

'Last year Britain's economy was very strong, but this year will be when the chickens come home to **roast**,' said Bootle.

What a difference one letter can make. The beauty of this eggcorn is that the consequence for 'chickens' when their 'chickens coming home to roost' is that they may well be roasted. Otherwise this is a new stage in convenience foods that the domesticated fowl is now so well trained that it comes home, turns the oven on and jumps inside once the temperature has reached 180° C. Now if there were such things as self-peeling potatoes life would have taken a large step forward.

Daily Telegraph

...having to wear glasses, doing exams, being sick, MRS MURIE!!!!! Ahhh she's off her **rocket**.

The origins of the phrase 'off her rocker' are slightly contentious but it is probably derived from the idea of a chair or cradle detached from the wooden arch-shaped runners which caused it to rock; hence, unstable or unreliable. However, there is a satisfyingly modern picture from the eggcorn 'off her rocket' which describes a wild-looking woman, waving frantically as she tumbles from a futuristic airplane.

🌱 Eggcorn   🍍 Malapropism   🦂 Mondegreen

I would have **roosted** but the floor was very dirty, and I wore my **peerless** blue jeans to **oppress** the hero.

Alex, one of the narrators of *Everything Is Illuminated*, kills the English language in a couple of different ways: both are displayed with some panache here. The first two words 'roosted' and 'peerless' are great examples of what I have called thesaurus abuse (see also ELECTRICAL and FLACCID); the third, 'oppress', reveals his talent for straightforward malapropism.

Jonathan Safran Foer, *Everything Is Illuminated*

 Then, from an entirely different perspective, some **rubble-rouser** like Jean-Marie Le Pen will come up with an inflammatory statement and single-handedly revive the discussion about the nature of Nazi occupation in the Second World War.

The refreshing thing about eggcorns is that they make you re-think your understanding of a word or phrase and they give you another image to work with in your head. So, while the traditional 'rabble-rouser' provoked a picture of a hot-headed, red-faced firebrand exhorting a volatile crowd, a rubble-rouser conjures the picture of someone trying to excite a group of people who, rubble-like, are rather less animated and excitable. That person has to be truly exceptionable to get a reaction.

chrenkoff.blogspot.com

 We just didn't have the **run of the mill**.

Glen Hoddle, supremely gifted footballer, former England coach and football pundit with a clairvoyant touch (he once commented 'his tackle was definitely pre-ordained'), mangled the normal 'run of the ball' and came up with something altogether more appropriate for the performance his side had just put in. Malapropisms sometimes show what's really going on in your mind and expose the truth you're trying to hide. Hoddle's team weren't victims of bad luck, they were just run of the mill.

Eggcorn   Malapropism   Mondegreen

Ss

Man, I mention my beef with the bike, and you so-called buddies **sail me down** the river!

The expression 'to sell down the river' originates in the US from before the abolition of slavery. It describes when a slave was sold to a plantation owner on the lower Mississippi where conditions were harsher than in the northern slave States. So the expression came to mean to betray or let down. 'Sail down the river' is an altogether less threatening saying which has connotations of a gentle Sunday afternoon boat trip along the Thames.

 Sandscript

Often heard for Sanskrit and of course all the better for it. Sanskrit is a pre-Classical era language of India whereas sandscript is simply the huge letters you write on the beach for passing planes to decipher – or at least it should be.

They haven't made many **sautées** forward.

Football pundits make 'sorties' into other languages at their peril. Clive Allen here attacks French with a will if not a dictionary and conjures the image of the footballer, skillet in hand, attempting to shallow fry the opposition.

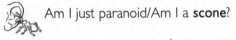 Am I just paranoid/Am I a **scone**?

Not much of a choice, I fear. Green Day's 1995 hit 'Basket Case' was about someone who thinks they're cracking up. It's not clear how some then make the random association with a scone but perhaps the randomness of the image fits in with the idea of an unhinged singer? Green Day actually sang 'Am I just paranoid/I'm just stoned'.

Green Day, 'Basket Case'

 Basically, it simulates the building, defending and con-
quering castles – from building, economic and military
perspectives. It has various types of play; a full campaign
(start from **scraps**, and follow the development of the
castle technology while you are at it).

'Scratch' is an old sporting term which derives from a line drawn in the ground from where a contest would begin (particularly in boxing). So it was a starting point and became a figurative expression for a position of no advantage or influence and from there a position of starting from nothing. If you start from 'scraps', however, you do have something, albeit the smallest amount of perhaps not very useful material. More *Ready, Steady, Cook* than *MasterChef*.

 It has a good climax and some wicked visuals, not really for the **screamish** but watchable.

This in an Amazon review of the horror film *Hollow Man* and it is a perfect example of an eggcorn – the word is immediately recognisable, it makes more sense in the context than the intended word ('squeamish') and adds a word to mainstream usage. I, for one, will happily use 'screamish' for any film from *Jaws* to *The Exorcist*. Another eggcorn in this area which would apply to a slightly different category of film (or television programme) is ***squirmish*** which is almost as good for those films which are either so embarrassing you wriggle in your seat or are so gory you cover your eyes.

🌱 Eggcorn　🌿 Malapropism　🐜 Mondegreen

This example comes from a review of *Pan's Labyrinth*: 'It is way more gory than I thought it would be, so if you are '**squirmish**' you may want to skip this one. Beyond that though, it's a really good film'. Both '**screamish**' and '**squirmish**' are excellent eggcorns which deserve mainstream use.

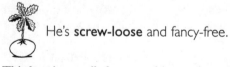

He's **screw-loose** and fancy-free.

This hasn't actually been used in any intentional way yet but is one to keep an eye on – it takes the freedom of footloose and adds a deranged element which has an appealingly dangerous edge to it. 'Screwloose' dates back to the early nineteenth century as a phrase to indicate a weakness in someone's 'mental faculties'. It astounds me that it has taken so long for it to be attached to 'fancy-free'.

Tonight I **sellotape my glove to** you.

Roberta Flack's moving and adoring love song takes a bizarre stationery twist. All couples have their secret rituals: Roberta's, according to some listeners, take a frankly odd form. She actually sang 'I celebrate my love for you' but I will forever have a soft-focus picture of the lovingly attached mitten.

Roberta Flack, 'Tonight I Celebrate My Love'

My **sensitive manatee** has gone down the drain.

Bob Dylan is more of a protestor than a natural historian; some people, though, clearly think he has a wide and exotic pet collection including in this instance the remarkable sea cow. He, by their reckoning at least, also has a very large sink. The singer was unavailable for comment. In fact, Dylan was singing that 'my sense of humanity has gone down the drain'.

Bob Dylan, 'Not Dark Yet'

Eggcorn   Malapropism   Mondegreen

Dirty deeds and they're done with **sheep**.

In the original song 'Dirty Deeds Done Dirt Cheap,' a man advertises his services to people with problems. He claims he can dispose of the 'problems' (usually people) in a variety of violent ways but in all cases 'dirt cheap'. In the mondegreen version (and a parody of the original has been written with this title), there is an extra even more unwelcome note of perversion in the song. I'm sure that AC/DC probably don't mind that at all.

AC/DC 'Dirty Deeds Done Dirt Cheap'

As you come down the **shoot** (about 50m long), you'll find yourself zipping along at a fast pace and the only eddy is on the right about half way down.

The words 'chute' and 'shoot' have actually been used fairly interchangeably in US and British English over the centuries. 'Chute' is an import from French which was adopted in the US while 'shoot' is from the Old English *scéotan*. Unusually, perhaps, the North American form is steadily disappearing. Expect more and more water 'shoots' in the coming years.

www.riversguidebook.co.uk

Beelzebub has a devil **for a sideboard**.

In 'Bohemian Rhapsody', Freddie Mercury teases us all with his baroque lyrics and his operatic delivery, turning the song into one of the most misheard (and therefore mis-sung) ever recorded. The song has attracted a lot of critical analysis as to its meaning but Mercury claimed it was just a load of 'random rhyming nonsense'. The nonsense part is important for all those who think that Beelzebub puts dishes, plates and other crockery on a devil. Why not? If you ask Scaramouche to do the fandango in a song, quite frankly you're asking for trouble. The actual lyric is 'Beelzebub has a devil put aside for me'. By the way, 'Bohemian Rhapsody' is the second most played single on British radio; it's just

Eggcorn   Malapropism   Mondegreen

behind that other much misheard blockbuster, *A Whiter Shade of Pale*. (***As the mirror told its tale*** is the most common mondegreen in that song but doesn't quite warrant a separate entry here.)

Queen, 'Bohemian Rhapsody'

I can find the **sink**, but not the **drain**.

Crowded House's 1991 single 'Weather With You' was their biggest success in the UK. The song describes an aspiring singer wandering about 57 Mount Pleasant Street but complaining 'things ain't cooking in my kitchen' which establishes the location and paves the way for the introduction of the sink and drain line in the mondegreen. However, this is one of those cases where a band's attempt at profundity is undermined by the mundane – the actual line is the nearly aphoristic 'I can find the sleep, but not the dream'. Sadly they have been misunderstood.

Crowded House, 'Weather With You'

However, in this situation, only library staff who have been designated as **'skeletal'** staff are asked to stay or come to work to keep buildings open and circulation services operating.

Often resources are stretched to the limit, so that an organisation can only field the smallest number of its employees to keep the business going; it is, in other words, operating with a skeleton staff. Things are really, really bad, though, if they start wasting away to become the bare bones only – not really a place you'd want to be working as part of a skeleton staff or not.

From the Cornell University Library
Inclement Weather Procedure

I'm not going to make a **skeptical** out of my boxing career.

Tonya Harding, ice-skater, wrestler, Internet celebrity – so many strings to her bow. Having moved on from ice-skating after an 'incident' at the US Figure Skating Championships in 1994 where she is alleged to have orchestrated the nobbling of her prime competitor,

Eggcorn   Malapropism   Mondegreen

Harding tried wrestling management before she took up the gloves. She made her professional debut on the undercard to another gaffe master, Mike Tyson, in 2003. Whether she made a 'spectacle' of herself, or whether she was 'skeptical' about her motives, isn't clear.

 Of course, if we were more in Scandinavia, we wouldn't be able to work in Germany, Poland and here. It was a blessing **in the skies**.

Or, indeed, in disguise. However, if you believe in divine help, then it is more likely to come from the skies than it is from an unlooked-for source.

www.buddhism.ru

 We don't want him to **smuthercate**.

A wonderful amalgam of smother and suffocate, 'smuthercate' demands immediate recognition from the OED. It is also ripe for eggcorning itself – 'smother Kate' anyone?

www.revise.com

I've been waiting for the **snowman** for all my life.

'In The Air Tonight' is probably the most famous of Phil Collins' solo singles. A mysterious, moody and enigmatic song which, as a result of its opaque lyrics, has been much interpreted and analysed. Collins himself, though, is quite happy to admit that he doesn't know what the song is about. So, why not send it over a surreal precipice and introduce a snowman in the climactic line? He actually sang 'I've been waiting for this moment for all my life' but in this version The Iceman Cometh …

Phil Collins, 'In the Air Tonight'

Eggcorn   Malapropism   Mondegreen

soak one's wild oats/oaks.

As an example of how we've moved away from the land, this expression comes up more and more compared with the original 'sow'. Where once we planted, nurtured and harvested, now we simply open the packet and add water.

 Kinky's **sorted** past is a magnet for Democrat voter.

A 'sorted' past can be one that is in good alphabetical (or chronological if you prefer) order or it can be one that is, in the style of The Offroaders from *The Fast Show*, dealt with, in fine shape. Neither meaning has anything to do with filthy, disgusting, gross actions or characters that the word 'sordid' describes.

blogs.chron.com

"Now honey, you know I only read the newspaper **spasmodically!**"

Some people get very agitated by the news media and others only read the newspaper from time to time. Maria Ruskin in the film of *The Bonfire of the Vanities* (played by Melanie Griffith) reads them 'periodically' but also in great pain by the sound of it.

 To be a leader, you have to develop **a spear de corps**.

But only in extreme circumstances I'm sure. *Esprit de corps* is one of those imported phrases whose moment seems to be passing. First used in the eighteenth century it is difficult to work out why the phrase is becoming rarer – whether the notion is old-fashioned or whether our education system simply doesn't include this kind of vocabulary. Whether it is down to one of these reasons or something else entirely, 'esprit de corps' is seldom seen or heard. Hence the need for some to reach out and grab a suitable, common alternative.

 Eggcorn   Malapropism   Mondegreen

'A spear de corps' is a compromise and I'm sure that we'll see a fully fledged English version in due course. In the meantime, we have 'a spear de corps' which sounds very uncomfortable.

www.langston.com

SONG TITLES

It takes a special kind of wilfulness to mishear a song title. More often than not when you hear a song you find out before or very shortly after what it is called. In 99.9 per cent of cases, the title will be included in the lyrics. (The main exception to this rule is the ten-minute prog-rock epic complete with drum and keyboard solos.) However, some people will carry on and create their own song titles using their ears as a guide. Here are some of the best:

Doughnuts Make My Brown Eyes Blue/Don't It Make My Brown Eyes Blue (Crystal Gale)

Mr Tangerine Man/'Mr Tamborine Man' (Bob Dylan)

Eyelids in the Street/'Islands in the Stream' (Kenny Rogers and Dolly Parton)

Gus Foster/'Ghostbusters' (Ray Parker Junior)

Sweet Dreams of Maitre D's/'Sweet Dreams (Are Made of This)' (Eurythmics)

You Make Me Feel Like a Man and a Woman/'(You Make Me) Feel Like a Natural Woman' (Aretha Franklin)

Flies in Outer Space/'Eyes Without a Face' (Billy Idol)

Diarrhoea/'Mamma Mia' (Abba)

Life in the Vaseline/'Life in the Fast Lane' (The Eagles)

Sue Lawley/'So Lonely' (The Police)

See also individual entries.

🌱 Eggcorn   🏛 Malapropism   🐑 Mondegreen

 **Stab in the liver**, your **mummy** or your **wife**.

Now that is what I call an ultimatum. Adam Ant's hit in 1981 had one of those videos that stick with you for life: it was a model of unrestrained exhibitionism with Adam dressed up as the 'dandy highwayman' cavorting about in full eighteenth-century regalia and clearly having the time of his life. What a shame that he wasn't aware of these alternative lyrics at the time: the extra dimension of a bit of liver-chopping would have been irresistible to the showman in him. What he actually sang was 'Stand and deliver, your money or your life'.

Adam and the Ants, 'Stand and Deliver'

 Can't Stand Gravy

k.d. lang's 1992 hit 'Constant Craving' remains her most famous song. It might have taken a nosedive in the charts if it had been retitled along the lines of this fantastic mishearing.

k.d. lang, 'Constant Craving'

 I'm in a complete **stagmire**.

A wonderful neologism from Little Carmine 'Brainless the Second' Lupertazzi in *The Sopranos*. Tony Soprano's relationship with the son of New York don Carmine Lupertazzi Snr is a strained one, particularly when Carmine Jnr starts to spout pretentious rubbish which is uncommonly linguistically twisted (Tony is himself hardly the 'pineapple' of competence). This one, though, is a stroke of genius as it combines to create a new word of strength and resonance. (And certainly better than if he'd combined stagnant and quagmire to produce 'quagnant' which doesn't work as well.)

The Sopranos

 How could I forget that I had given her an **STD**?

When Shaggy's friend comes to him for advice because he has been caught 'red-handed' with the girl next door by his girlfriend, there seems no way out. His girlfriend managed to catch him because he had given 'her an extra key'. Not, as some people hear, the more

🌱 Eggcorn   📚 Malapropism   🐜 Mondegreen

serious STD in which case she would have double cause for complaint. Shaggy's advice, by the way, 'Never admit to a word when she say makes a claim' is unhelpful in either case.

Shaggy, 'Wasn't Me'

 It was a **stone-bonking** penalty.

Ouch. Niall Quinn expresses his outrage at the injustice of a referee's decision in such a way that it is probably best not to dwell on it further. With or without the Kenneth Williams factor, it's not a picture you want to call up too often. Footballers use the adjective 'stonewall' for a penalty that should have been given but is not.

star-craving mad.

In our celebrity-obsessed times this mishearing seems particularly apt. While in previous eras, simply being 'stark-raving' mad meant to be utterly insane, the expression can now be seen to be applied to those who specifically have a mania for the famous. A stalker perhaps or someone who has a subscription to *Hello*. The expression can rightly be used for those braving the elements to boo at the ejected *Celebrity Big Brother* housemates on a stormy night in January. They really are 'star-craving mad'. The expression has also been used for the title of a film in 2002.

Are you going to **starve an old friend?**

'Scarborough Fair' is one of those songs about which a huge amount has been written – not only about its origins but also about the symbolism and hidden meaning of the lyrics. Debate simmers (it's not a particularly heated argument) about the symbolism of 'parsley, sage, rosemary and thyme'. The first line of course is actually 'Are you going to Scarborough Fair?' In this version, though, academic debate is pointless – there's a blunt question which requires an immediate answer.

Simon and Garfunkel, 'Scarborough Fair'

🌱 Eggcorn   🌿 Malapropism   🐜 Mondegreen

More **subliminal** skills from Nakamura.

Football commentators are famous for playing fast and loose with the English language – a skill which becomes ever more pronounced as the excitement of a match builds. This example from BBC Radio Scotland is, well, 'sublime'. The OED defines 'subliminal' as 'Below the threshold of sensation or consciousness' which positively begs for the commentator to follow this utterance up with 'as he ghosts past another player'. Happily he didn't or it would not have appeared in this book.

And you come to me on a **submarine**.

From the Bee Gees' 'How Deep Is Your Love?' If some listeners are to be believed, it can be as deep as a man-made submersible will go. The actual lyrics are: 'And you come to me on a summer breeze/Keep me warm in your love and then softly leave.' But as a gesture of unshakeable love, arriving in a submarine is pretty much up there with the best.

The Bee Gees, 'How Deep Is Your Love?'

The Pinball Wizard has **suction cups for** wrists.

Tommy, the Pinball Wizard, in The Who's rock opera was deaf, dumb and blind which made his prowess at the pinball machine all the more remarkable. Perhaps the addition of suction cups made using the flippers easier and gave him the advantage of his opponents? Given the psychedelic atmosphere of the film, those wrists wouldn't have looked out of place. The Who actually sang that he had 'such a supple wrist' which is much less interesting.

The Who, 'Pinball Wizard'

Eggcorn   Malapropism   Mondegreen

The Ants Are My Friends 137

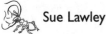 Sue Lawley

A very famous mishearing of the classic 1978 Police song 'So Lonely'. At the time Sue Lawley was presenting Nationwide with Frank Bough before going on to be the BBC's anchor newsreader and presenter of Desert Island Discs. The song is about someone who has lost the only person he can ever love; in some ears that can only mean Sue Lawley.

The Police, 'So Lonely'

 Because of a transmission error, an interview in the Egos & Ids column on May 16 with Mary Matalin, the former deputy manager of the Bush campaign who is a co-host of a new talk show on CNBC, quoted her incorrectly on the talk show host Rush Limbaugh. She said he was **'sui generis,'** not 'sweet, generous.'

Even the most prestigious news organisations can get things horribly wrong. Here, rather than damn Rush Limbaugh (the notorious right-wing American political shockjock) with faint praise as being 'one of a kind', Mary Matalin's comments come out in the *New York Times* as the very patronising 'sweet, generous'.

 Michelle, ma belle, **Sunday monkey play no piano song, no piano song**.

Sometimes when you're faced with a foreign language in a song, it's just too much effort to try to decipher the lyrics. There is perhaps the occasional word that rings a bell but, quite frankly, why bother trying to work it all out? Such are the thoughts of some listeners when they hear *Michelle*. So, sadly, the 'Sunday Monkey' (ah yes – *that* monkey) doesn't play a 'piano song' – a source of great disappointment to us all I'm sure. If only he would, our lives would be fuller. However, more careful listeners to the song will have realised that the translation of the French appears in the previous verse. No mention of monkeys or songs. Just words that 'go together well' ('très bien ensemble').

The Beatles, 'Michelle'

🌱 Eggcorn　🍍 Malapropism　🐜 Mondegreen

There is no **surefool** way of proceeding.

Well, perhaps there is if you want to be wrong? To act in a surefool way presumably means that you are bound to get it wrong – it's surefire or foolproof that you will do so. Incompetent, inept and foolish behaviour now has a nice adjective.

It was a definite penalty but Wright made a right **swan-song** of it.

Another gaffe-prone manager-turned-pundit, Jack Charlton, baffles to deceive here. He meant, I think, that Wright made a right 'song and dance' of it; but I could be wrong, and he really did mean that Wright suffered a career-ending injury but came back on briefly for a last hurrah.

Sweet Dreams of Maitre D's

A variation of the food themed 'made of CHEESE', this mishearing of one of the most famous Eurythmics songs has an appealing fetishistic quality. Those who dream of the authoritarian, rather condescending image of the man running the restaurant can now sing a hymn of praise to him.

Eurythmics, 'Sweet Dreams (Are Made of This)'

 Eggcorn   Malapropism   Mondegreen

Amazon's **tangenital** references.

This from a blog pointing out that Amazon's recommendations system can go wrong. Other instances have people mis-saying the word 'tangential' for a number of years. However, as nude sun-bathing is legal, there is every reason for the word's existence – so 'tan-genital' should be embraced as a useful addition to the dictionary.

Hey, Mr **Tangerine** Man

There are many theories as to the origins and meaning of Bob Dylan's 1964 song, 'Mr Tambourine Man': some think it deals with his experiments with LSD while others see the inspiration as Bruce Langhorne who used a huge Turkish tambourine-like drum in his performance. It was actually a hit first for The Byrds who recorded a version of it in 1965 which reached Number One in the US Billboard Chart. It's been covered many times but perhaps the most unlooked-for version is by William Shatner (aka Captain Kirk) who recorded his spoken-word cover to the same critical acclaim as his rendition of 'Lucy in the Sky with Diamonds'. The tangerine mishearing of this great anthem is, of course, much more prescient now, with celebrities applying liberal doses of self-tanning cream to give themselves a distinctive orange glow.

Bob Dylan, 'Mr Tambourine Man'

So you wanna make a **tapestry**.

The anthem 'We Haven't Turned Around' on Gomez's album *Liquid Skin* conjures apocalyptic scenarios of death and destruction. The real lyric invites the listener to 'make catastrophe'; some of the audience want to stay on much safer, domestic territory and hear 'tapestry'. I don't blame them.

Gomez, 'We Haven't Turned Around'

 There's the man I chose, There's my **Teletubby**.

Shakira's extraordinary career as dancer, writer, songwriter, actor and internationally renowned pop singer also embraces being a Goodwill Ambassador for UNICEF. Perhaps that is why some people hear 'Teletubby' instead of 'territory' in 'Underneath Your Clothes'?

Shakira, 'Underneath Your Clothes'

 Fine furniture at reasonable prices: antique, colonial, and **temporary**.

If you are unsure about buying a cookbook for which recipes and their ANTIDOTES are supplied, buying 'fine furniture' from this supplier might be a gamble as well. The writer meant 'contemporary'.

 It's good to be back on the old **terracotta**.

Del Boy has an armoury of foreign words and phrases at his disposal which he uses as moments of high drama. Del Boy was stretching for 'terra firma' in this case. In other episodes he exclaims 'Fromage frais' or 'Chateauneuf du Pape' if something is really serious; and in situations where he is helpless and life just deals him a bad hand, 'al dente' or 'Allemagne dix points' are, pardon me, trotted out.

Only Fools and Horses

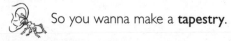 Eggcorn   Malapropism   Mondegreen

That singer before me. Who was HE? It was very coura-geous of MTV to start the show with a genuine, how you say ... transvestite. He was very convincing. It was only his hands and his **testi satchels** that gave it away.

A new take on men's anatomy and indeed, on Madonna (the singer before him) by Borat, the creation of Sacha Baron Cohen. As satchels are normally slung over the shoulder this is a particularly excruciating image and one that demands no further explanation.

 Our first goal was pure **textile**.

John Lambie, three-time manager and saviour of Scottish football club Partick Thistle (also known as the 'Great Lambini' apparently), should be entered into the Malaprop Hall of Fame for this one. Missing the ending of 'textbook' he careened straight into the haberdashery department and grabbed whatever he could find. In this case, it sounds like a criticism: while 'a textbook goal' may be one to savour, 'a textile goal' is fabricated and therefore didn't come naturally. Fans of Partick Thistle probably couldn't care less.

I was sick and tired of **being thin**/When I called you last night from **Tesco**.

The original line, 'I was sick and tired of everything/When I called you last night from Glasgow,' isn't much of a set-up for the song; much better is this misheard line which conjures an intriguing backstory of excessive dieting (why?), a crisis in the narrator's life (what provoked it?) and a full shopping trolley at the nation's biggest supermarket. The supermarket sweep in the ice-cream section is about to begin when she calls her friend to confess all. Now, that is what I call the beginning to a song.

Abba, 'Super Trouper'

🌱 Eggcorn   🌿 Malapropism   🦂 Mondegreen

Wouldn't it be nice if we were older, then we wouldn't have to wear a **thong**.

The Beach Boys classic album *Pet Sounds* is still one of pop music's greatest achievements. The song 'Wouldn't It Be Nice?' is the opening song on it and sets off the album which is about teenage life unfolding and an exciting future ahead. The song though dwells on how at that stage of your life nothing can happen quickly enough. It is news to me that as a teenager you *were forced* to wear a thong although some people believe that is what Brian Wilson was singing. In fact he sang 'then we wouldn't have to wait too long'. Phew!

The Beach Boys, 'Wouldn't It Be Nice?'

It was all hugely entertaining and, one suspects, very much **thumb in cheek**.

Speaking with your 'tongue in your cheek' has been a description of insincerity or sly irony since the mid-eighteenth century. The slyness is the important aspect of this phrase because with your tongue in your cheek you make a relatively inconspicuous visual gesture to indicate that what you're saying is not exactly what you mean. If, however, you stick your thumb in your cheek, you're pretty much shouting out something – what, nobody will know, because it will be utterly incomprehensible.

The Independent

Rocket man, burning all the **trees off every** lawn.

This mishearing of the Elton John classic 'Rocket Man' paints a satisfying cartoon picture of our hero flying low over the Earth, scorching domestic gardens as he goes. In fact the song is about a Mars-bound astronaut and his feelings of leaving his family back on Earth – no mention of his own garden and none of burnt trees. The actual words are 'Rocket man, burning out his fuse up here alone'.

Elton John, 'Rocket Man'

Eggcorn   Malapropism   Mondegreen

TOP TEN MALAPROPISMS

1. *Barbarous Monster! How have I deserved that my Passion should be resulted and treated with* **Ironing**.
2. *If we're going to maintain America's status as the number one maritime power ... it means having modern* **musicians** *and well-trained soldiers.*
3. *He is the very* **pineapple** *of politeness.*
4. *You'll have to come up to date and have microphones, Vicar. The* **agnostics** *in this church are very poor.*
5. *Because of a transmission error, an interview in the Egos & Ids column on May 16 with Mary Matalin, the former deputy manager of the Bush campaign who is a co-host of a new talk show on CNBC, quoted her incorrectly on the talk show host Rush Limbaugh. She said he was '**sui generis**' not 'sweet, generous'. Corrections, New York Times, 29 May 1993*
6. *This is not a game for the* **puritans**.
7. *Don't ever wear yellow, dear. It makes your skin look shallow and* **emancipated**.
8. *It's a proven fact that Capital Punishment is a* **detergent** *for crime.*
9. *There's a great* **harmonium** *in the dressing room.*
10. '*There she identically goes! Poor sweet young creetur, there she goes, like a lamb to the sacrifge! If there's any illness when that wessel gets to sea,' said Mrs Gamp, prophetically, 'it's murder, and I'm the witness for the* **persecution**.'

We're **courting a trout**, I can't walk out.

Elvis had some unusual habits and obsessions: making eyes at fish was not one of them as far as I'm aware. However, some people mishear 'we're caught in a trap' as precisely this and I welcome their mishearing. It brings a whole new slant to a great song which now describes two people, one of whom is deeply in love with the other,

Eggcorn   Malapropism   Mondegreen

and the other who is sadly besotted with freshwater fish. An unusual theme for a pop song but who would have thought that a song about a puppet on a string or indeed two little boys would have reached Number One either?

Elvis Presley, 'Suspicious Minds'

Uu

I've seen some bad tackles, but that was the **ultimatum**.

Alan Mullery is responsible for this malapropism in which he conjures the image of the defender approaching the player with the ball and shouting 'Give me the ball or else!' I'm sure that in these days where any physical contact is deemed a foul, the FA would probably welcome this extension of the defender's art. If they could make football entirely non-contact I'm sure they would.

All identifying details have been disguised in order to preserve **unanimity**.

While the social worker who wrote this report is doing his best to be fair, in fact this misuse of 'unanimity' can be construed to be anything but fair. 'Preserving unanimity' is the goal of many in delicate political situations involving complex negotiations with people from lots of different sides of a dispute; but it is not something to be wished for where justice is required. The author of the report meant 'anonymity', I'm sure.

This is **unparalysed** in the State's history

Whether it is 'unparalysed' or not, it is certainly unparalleled. This is a quote from Gib Lewis, Speaker of the Texas House of

Representatives. I like the idea that whatever it was has now been miraculously freed from its state of paralysis. Lewis is also responsible for a couple of other fine malapropisms. Speaking after his inauguration as Speaker of the Texas House for the fifth time he touchingly (and damply) commented, 'I am filled with humidity'; and, not being able to make his mind up on a particularly thorny issue he said, 'There's a lot of uncertainty that's not clear in my mind.'

 Eggcorn   Malapropism   Mondegreen

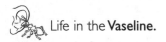 Life in the **Vaseline.**

This mishearing appeals simply because it contradicts the actual title of the song 'Life in the Fast Lane' so completely. While The Eagles depicted two people in a relationship, each living on the edge with wild parties and copious amounts of sex and drugs, some people think that it's a song about being stuck in a slippery, yet very thick, gel. Either way the song's next line 'Surely make you lose your mind' is appropriate.

The Eagles, 'Life in the Fast Lane'

 It should be noted for the comfort of those wishing to look at the devastation at a required safe distance, that although St. George's Hill provides a real **vintage** point, Richmond Hill is not far behind.

This from a reporter when the Soufriere Hills Volcano on Montserrat was exuding lava in late 1999. As well as referring to a particular year's crop of wine, vintage can also refer to the harvest of the wine and 'a vintage point' would be the place in which this is done. In other circumstances a useful extra to the language: in the midst of a volcanic 'incident' viticulture might be the last thing on your mind.

Montserrat Reporter

When Smokey sings/I fear **violence**.

I happen to be a huge fan of Smokey Robinson and have always thought of him as a benign musical influence. Some people, though, think that ABC are voicing their dread of Robinson in the song 'When Smokey Sings'. In fact what they sang was 'I hear violins' which is much more like it.

ABC, 'When Smokey Sings'

Eggcorn   Malapropism   Mondegreen

Ww–Zz

 Waltzing bright and beautiful.

Strictly Come Dancing has a lot to answer for – Peter Schmeichel's Samba is one memory which still needs suppressing – but it can't be blamed for this mishearing of the traditional hymn 'All Things Bright and Beautiful'. That said, waltzing can be bright and beautiful …

'All Things Bright and Beautiful'

I have **a watch, I have it on-n-n-n**.

Another mondegreen in the category of dragging in the everyday when the singer had something much more epic in mind. The singer in 'I Am a Rock' is clearly a jilted lover proclaiming how resilient he is and how he does not need friendship or contact with the outside world. Grand themes with lots of stone, wall and rock images. Some people, though, miss this altogether and hear him angrily declare that he has a timepiece *and* he is wearing it. That really told the world where to get off. Some people hear the next line – signalling even more defiance and sneering at the world – that 'a watch feels no pain'. Something no one will dispute. Simon and Garfunkel actually sing 'I am a rock, I am an island, and a rock feels no pain'.

Simon and Garfunkel, 'The Sound of Silence'

TOP TEN MONDEGREENS

This selection is based on nothing but my own opinion – I speak as someone with no more right to compile a mondegreen top ten than anyone else. I've selected the ones I think conjure a complete but different picture from the one intended by the songwriter and examples where the misheard lyric utterly undermines or changes the tone of a song.

1. *Israeli men! Hallelujah! Israeli men* – The Weather Girls' one-hit wonder 'It's Raining Men' deserves top spot just because I think it's very funny.
2. *You don't have to say you love me just* **because I'm mad** – an unnerving threat if ever there was one. Dusty Springfield's classic is given a slightly psychotic twist.
3. *Then I saw her face, now I'm* **gonna leave her** – a first rate of example of ignoring the emotional intelligence of a song.
4. *I've* **got the runs** *like a rolling bolt of thunder* – oh! what a night indeed.
5. *Tonight I* **sellotape** *my glove to you* – it's a gesture, I suppose, of undying love but not the most romantic I've ever heard.
6. **The ants** *are my friends, / they're blowin' in the wind /* **The ant**s *are a-blowin' in the wind* – Bob Dylan's classic is given an entomological make-over.
7. *I can see* **Cleveland now, Lorraine** *has gone* – the double mondegreen and the image of a huge Lorraine departing, allowing the singer to see Cleveland does it for me.
8. *Deck the halls with* **Buddy Holly** – why not indeed?
9. *No* **Dukes of Hazard** *in the classroom / Teacher leave them* **Dukes** *alone!* – This scrapes in ahead of so many others because it undermines the pompous Pink Floyd's sombre message.
10. *If you wanna be my* **plumber** – The Spice Girls' glamour will never be the same again.

Eggcorn   Malapropism   Mondegreen

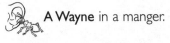 **A Wayne** in a manger.

Gervase Phinn published a book of 'the things children say' with this title in 2005. The story goes that a teacher was attempting to tell the nativity story to a class of children when he hit a stonewall in the form of a boy who insisted that the baby's name was Wayne, not Jesus. When pushed the mishearing of 'Away in a manger' above was the explanation. The rewriting of Christian history with Wayne as the central player is a tempting proposition. Instead of Jesus 'The Anointed One' bringing the dead back to life and turning water into wine, we have Wayne (which means 'The Wagon Builder') preaching 4–4–2 and the complete lyrics of *Oliver*. Banners at football matches displaying John 11:35 would translate as 'Wayne wept'. Manchester United supporters rejoice: your striker walks on water.

Gervase Phinn, *A Wayne in a Manger*

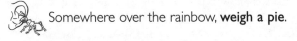 Somewhere over the rainbow, **weigh a pie**.

One of the things that I don't remember seeing when the tornado hits Judy Garland's farm in *The Wizard of Oz* is a pie. So how people think when she gets to the place over the rainbow she is going to weigh one is beyond me. Still, it's a more interesting image than the original 'way up high'.

Judy Garland, 'Somewhere Over the Rainbow'

 Scientologists **weld** a lot of power, enough to challenge the US and other world governments in court and win.

If you're talking political or corporate machismo, you could do worse than mishear 'weld' for 'wield'. In this context, the board room becomes a testosterone-fuelled (forgive me) high-octane environment where men do men things and, well, stick pieces of metal together with a hot candle.

🌴 Eggcorn   🍍 Malapropism   🐜 Mondegreen

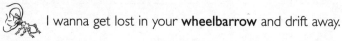 I wanna get lost in your **wheelbarrow** and drift away.

Following hard on the heels of the (misheard) refrain 'give me the **Beach Boys**', this mondegreen pushes 'Drift Away' into the realms of the absurd. Having dealt with the image of the California kings of surf, if you're mishearing right, you'll end up in a Tardis of a wheelbarrow and be cast off to sea. What he actually sang was 'I wanna get lost in your rock and roll'.

Dobie Gray, 'Drift Away'

 Everybody in a **wholesale frock**.

While Elvis Presley gyrated his way around the prison block, some people think he may have been having a slightly surreal moment by seeing the prisoners wearing the equivalent of TK Maxx dresses. Seems unlikely somehow but with Elvis you never can tell. The original was simply 'everybody in the whole cell block'.

Elvis Presley, 'Jailhouse Rock'

 We-Ping is getting fat. She was sitting on the dining room **windowseal** last night.

Sill (in window-sill) is an extremely old word meaning a horizontal timber supporting a wall or other structure. It's only common use now is in window- and doorsill but both instances are increasingly rare. So, naturally, we reach out for similar sounding alternatives and window-seal is a good one. As the ad says, 'it does exactly what it says on the tin'.

Oh what joy, this hibiscus bloom has brought to me during this frigidly cold winter that we are experiencing. With the **windshield** factor, it is minus 41 below zero Farenheit in lovely southwestern Quebec.

If the windchill factor is taken into account then presumably it is even colder?

www.gardenbuddies.com

 Eggcorn   Malapropism   Mondegreen

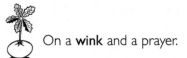 On a **wink** and a prayer.

The original phrase 'a wing and a prayer' comes from a song written in 1943 called 'Coming in on a Wing and a Prayer' which describes a wartime plane landing with only one wing after a successful mission. This version of it is rather more coy and knowing and so is equally useful. There is one further variation which provides for an altogether more spontaneous situation which is on 'a whim and a prayer'.

Oh, she may get **woolly**, women do get woolly, because of **all the stress**.

Otis Redding's version of the song is mondegreened brilliantly by Tim Robbins' character (Nuke LaLoosh) in the film *Bull Durham*. He murders the guitar parts as well, much to the annoyance of Kevin Costner who plays the experienced, cynical hack to Robbins' naïve, arrogant prodigy. LaLoosh goes on to give a lot of women a lot of stress in the film. The actual lines are: 'Ooh she may be weary, And them young girls they do get weary, wearing that same old shaggy dress'.

Otis Redding, 'Try a Little Tenderness'

 … [He] is a true gentlemen and **work alcoholic** to the cause.

This is becoming more commonplace as the health risks of work and alcohol become more apparent. Famously it was also said by the former Liverpool manager Gerard Houllier of Sir Alex Ferguson, the manager of Manchester United. It is unusual for a two-word phrase to be formed where there is an established single word. So, we have 'workaholic' (and even the noun 'workaholism') which has been around since the late 1960s; perhaps the inadvertent intention here is to intensify the negative tone of the original.

Eggcorn   Malapropism   Mondegreen

Wrangle an invitation.

The OED defines the verb 'wrangle' as 'To dispute angrily; to argue noisily or vehemently; to altercate, contend; to bicker', while 'wangle' is 'to accomplish (something) in an irregular way by scheming or contrivance'. We live in an impolite, abrupt world, 'wrangle' is much more appropriate.

 For example, there's a pensive, suspender-wearing TV host named Barry King, who is a dead **wringer** for CNN's Larry King.

The word 'wringer' comes from an Old High German word meaning 'wrestler' and still has the sense of someone who pressurises (and by extension therefore oppresses) another. The original phrase 'dead ringer' is an American sporting slang term which the OED dates back to the early 1890s and means to resemble so closely as to be indistinguishable. Perhaps 'dead wringer' is a violent impostor who has had his come-uppance?

USA Today

 We built this city on the **wrong damn road**.

There are times to regret an action, and there are times to keep quiet. If this misheard lyric is anything to go by then this almighty cock-up is best left to fester in some municipal vault somewhere – presumably in the Planning Department. 'We Built This City' was recently awarded 'The Number 1 Awesomely Bad Song Ever' by *Blender* magazine. The editors of the magazine decided it was so clearly a product of crass corporate commercialism despite purporting to be a diatribe against big music corporations that it merited the award. The original lyrics are 'We built this city of Rock and Roll'. Perhaps the blander misheard lyric would have been a better option after all?

Starship, 'We Built This City'

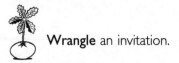 Eggcorn   Malapropism   Mondegreen

WILLIAM SHAKESPEARE

Shakespeare was an inveterate malapropist – he used it to great effect to undermine the comic and pompous characters he created. One terrific ping-pong malaprop scene in *The Merchant of Venice* has Launcelot Gobbo and his father (Old Gobbo) soliciting Bassanio to allow Launcelot to join his father as a servant to Bassanio. They interrupt and overlap the request and misuse words at crucial moments in each sentence:

GOBBO: He hath a great *infection*, sir, as one would say, to serve …

LAUNCELOT: Indeed, the short and the long is, I serve the Jew, and have a desire, as my father shall specify …

GOBBO: His master and he, saving your worship's reverence, are scare cater-cousins.

LAUNCELOT: To be brief, the very truth is that the Jew having done me wrong doth cause me, as my father, being I hope an old man, shall *frutify* unto you …

GOBBO: I have here a dish of doves that I would bestow upon your worship, and my suit is …

LAUNCELOT: In very brief, sir, the suit is *impertinent* to myself, as your worship shall know by this honest old man, and though I say it, though old man, yet poor man, my father …

BASSANIO: One speak for both. What would you?

LAUNCELOT: Serve you, sir.

GOBBO: That is the very *defect* of the matter, sir.

Gobbo's last malapropism underlines the absurd figures they cut in their supplication to Bassanio. It's a great scene which shows how brilliantly Shakespeare can use this kind of wordplay to undermine the characters so well even as they speak.

🌱 Eggcorn   🐜 Malapropism   🐜 Mondegreen

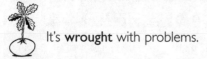

It's **wrought** with problems.

Normally, we'd say that something is 'fraught with difficulty or problems' where 'fraught' means 'laden' (like a ship – fraught is related to 'freight') and 'fraught with' then holds out the idea that something (an approach, an idea) is carrying with it as attribute; so 'a project fraught with complexity' means that it has the promise of being a complex project. However, if something is 'wrought' with problems then there is no promise of it being problematic: it is in its very make-up problematic. A subtle but very useful variation which is being taken up more and more.

SELECT BIBLIOGRAPHY

I used the Arden editions of Shakespeare throughout. The OED as always is the most invaluable resource. Other books consulted are:

Jonathan Coe, *What a Carve Up!* (London, 1995)

David Crystal, *The Stories of English* (London, 2004)

Anne Fadiman, *Ex Libris* (London, 2000)

Jonathan Safran Foer, *Everything Is Illuminated*, (London, 2003)

Elizabeth Knowles (ed.), *The Oxford Dictionary of Quotations* (Oxford, 2004)

Richard Lederer, *Anguished English* (USA, 2006)

OTHER SOURCES

If you want to delve deeper into the world of mondegreens, malapropisms and eggcorns, try the following places:

www.kissthisguy.com – The Archive of Misheard Lyrics. A spectacularly good and growing collection of mondegreens

www.amiright.com – slightly more hit and miss but there are some real gems here if you persevere. The site also provides the opportunity to create your own parodies of famous bands and musicians.

www.iusedtobelieve.com/music/misheard_lyrics – again worth checking out if you have the time. You can search by star-rating which makes the process easier.

Lots of great word-related websites will help you explore the language mistake world:

eggcorns.lascribe.net is the best place to look for the burgeoning number of eggcorns. Michael Quinion's World Wide Words is a good place for definitions and he is excellent at responding to questions about specific words and phrases. The newspaper corrections and clarification columns are always worth perusing and finally the OED is, of course, invaluable for research and citations.